I0477632

This Coloring Book Belongs To:

Color Chart

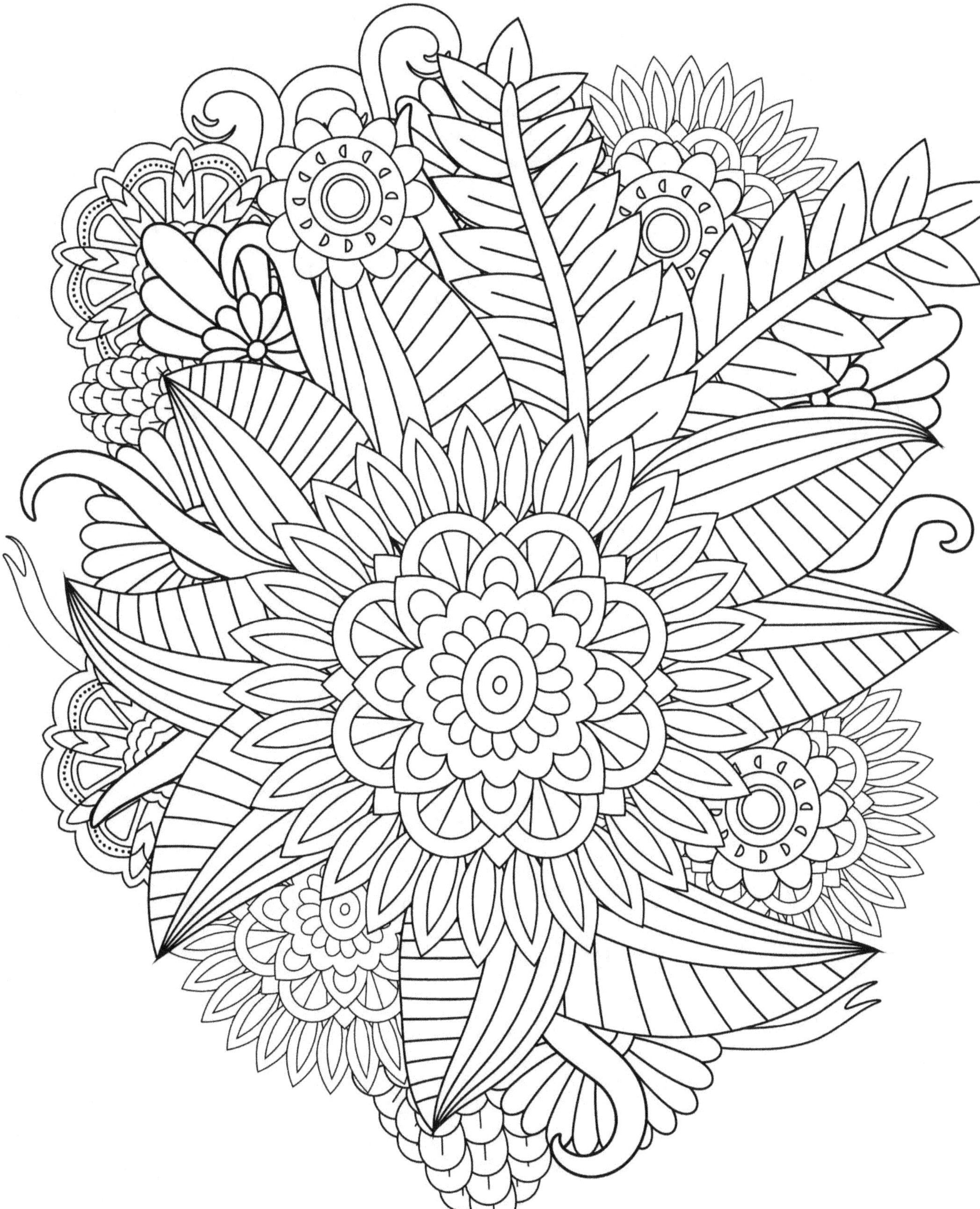

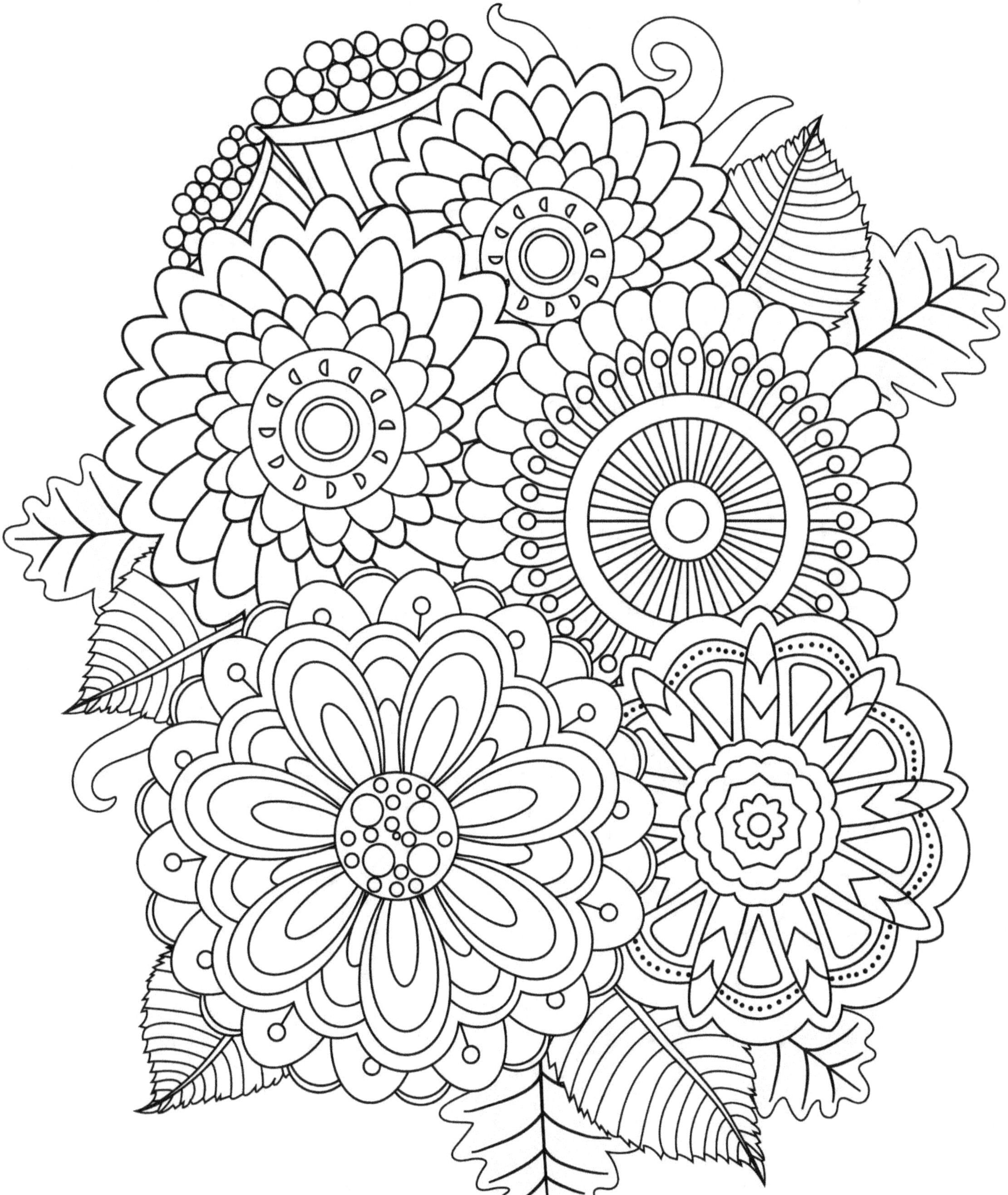

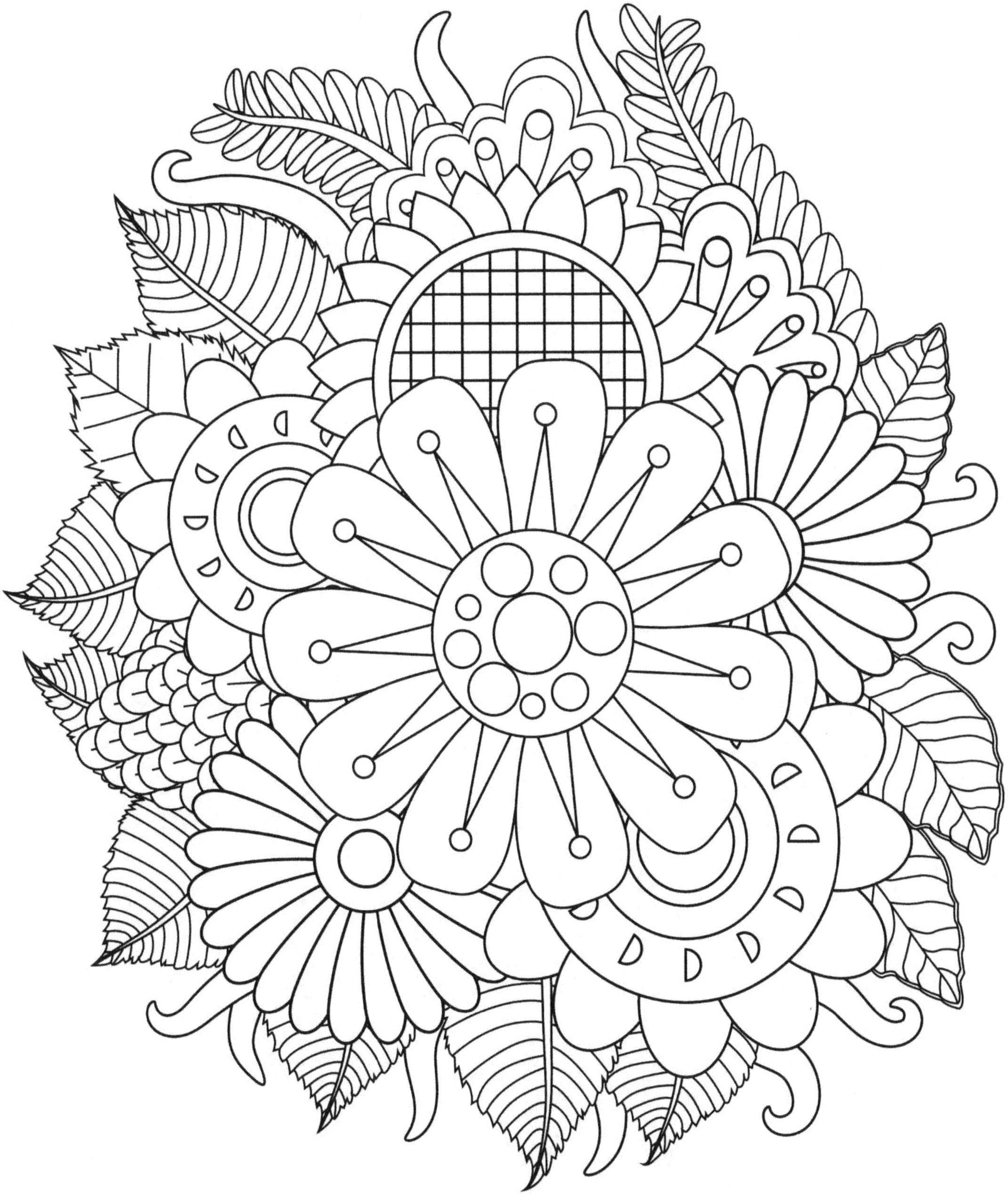

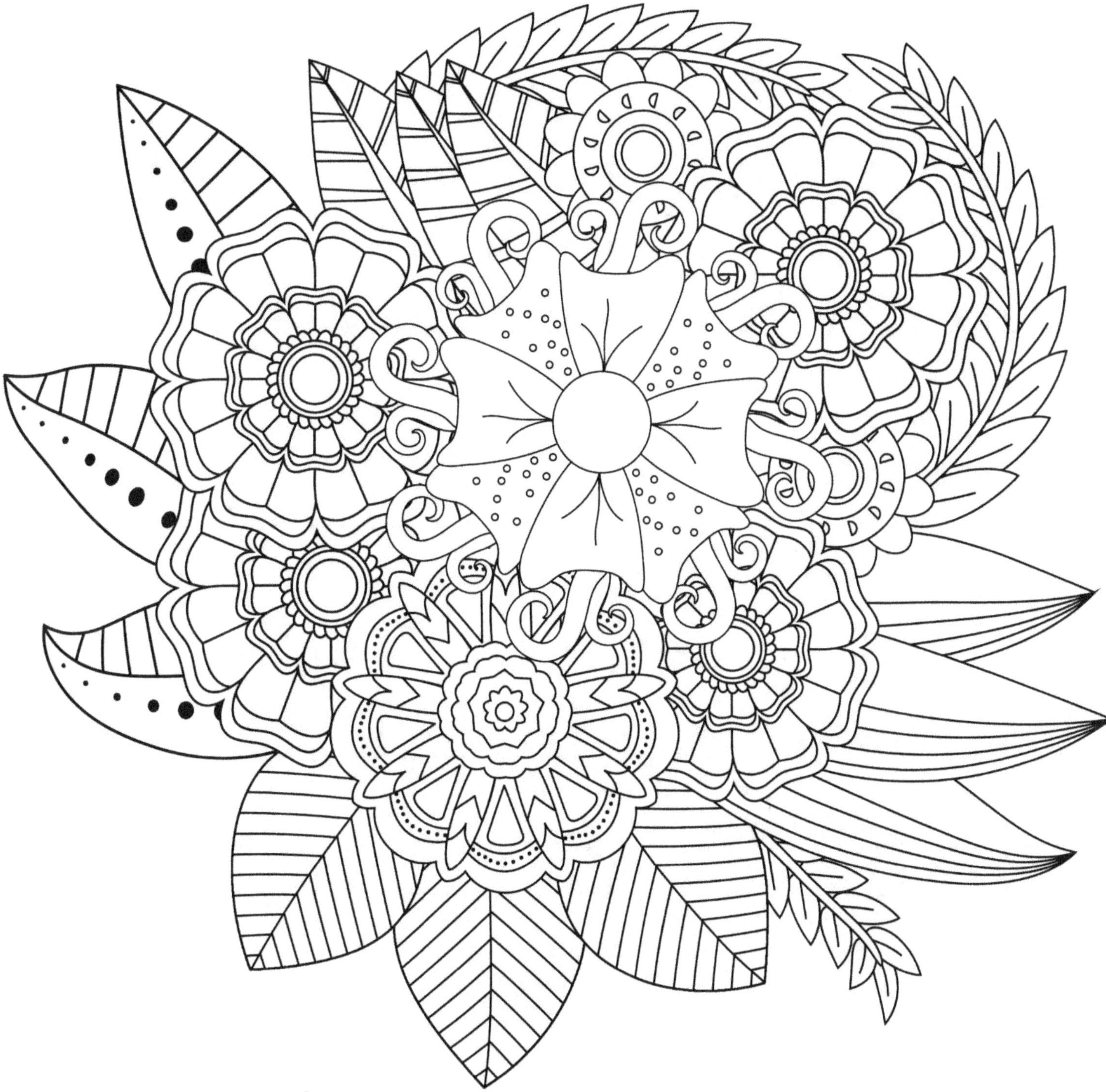

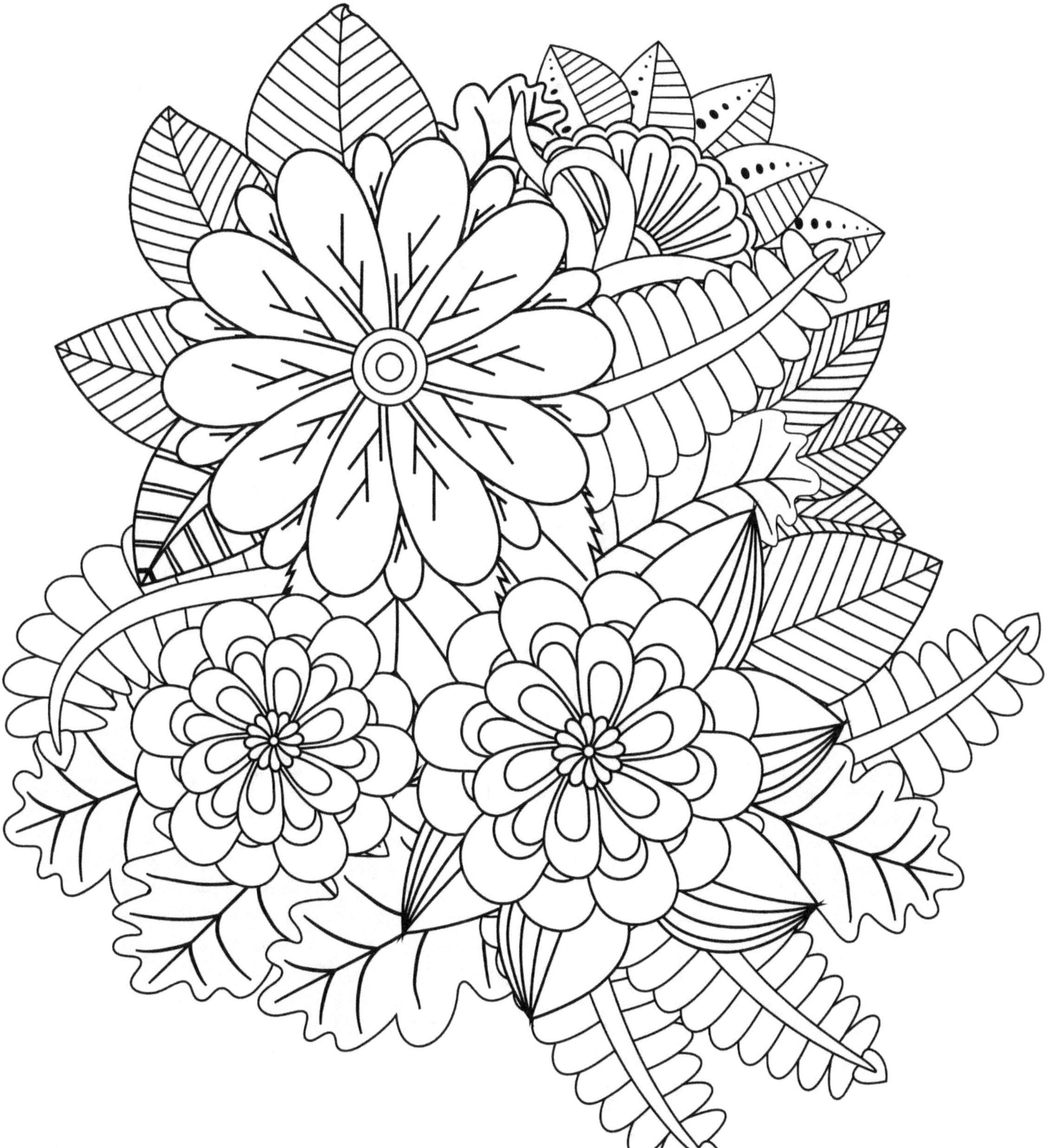

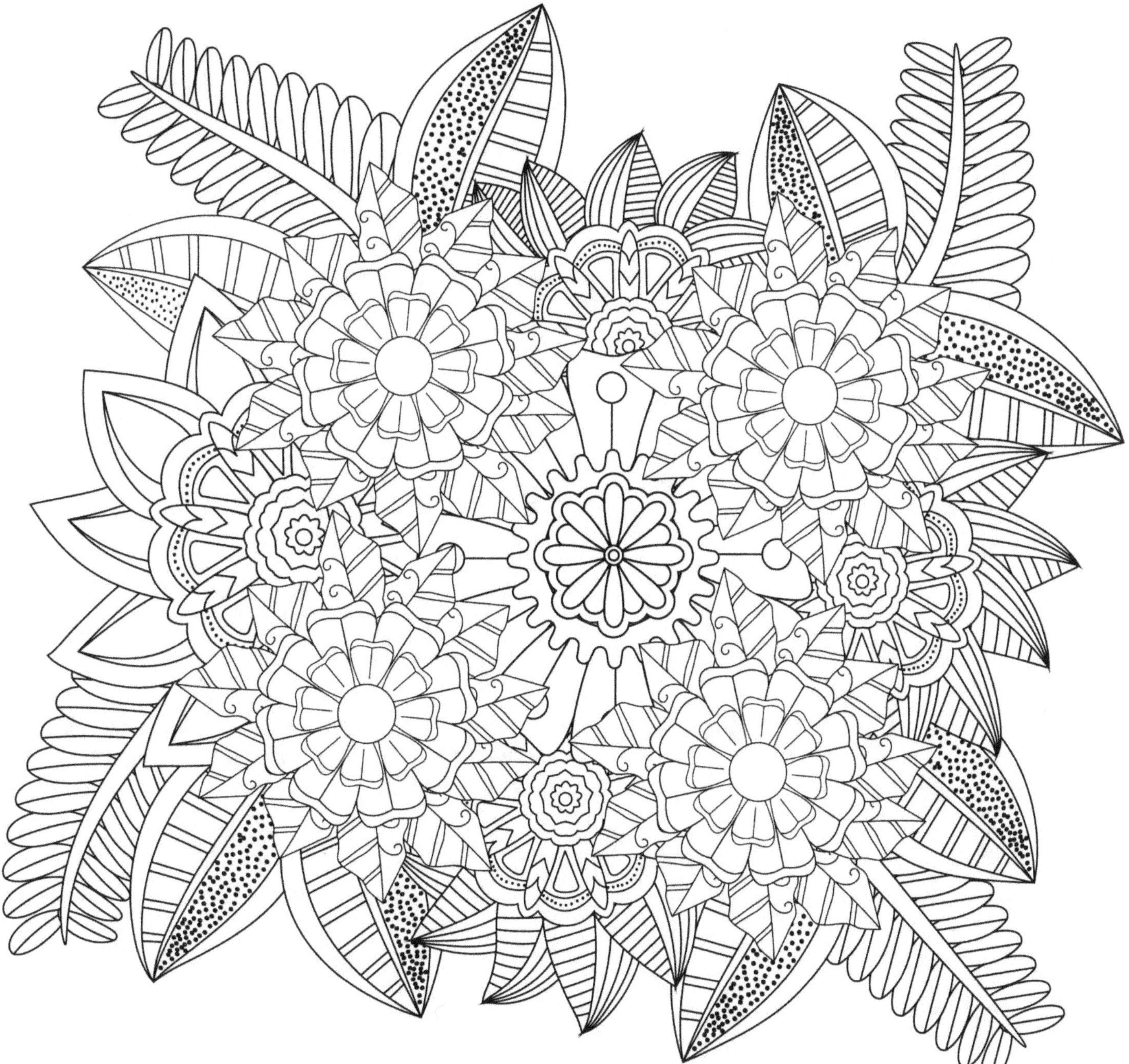

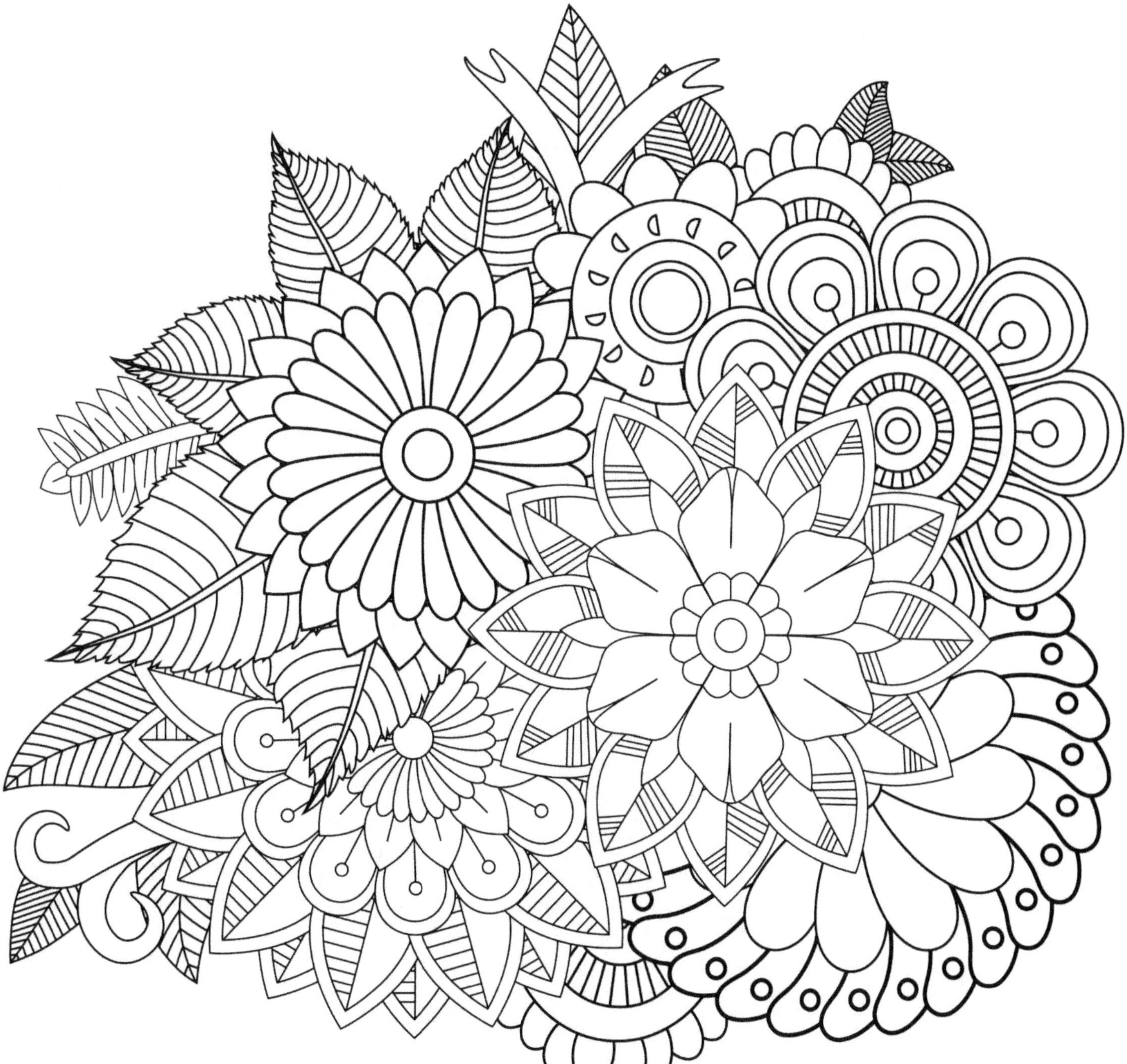

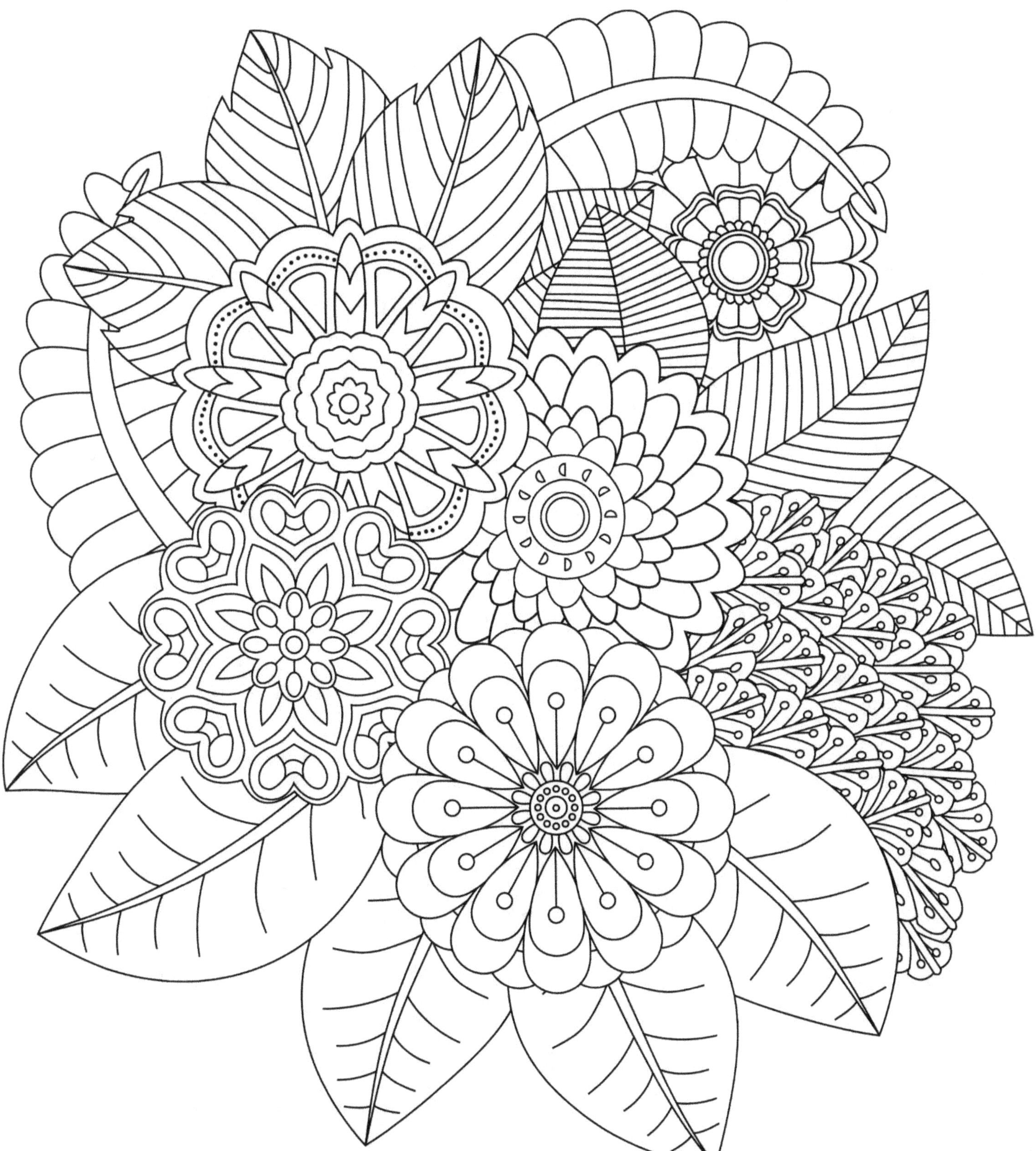

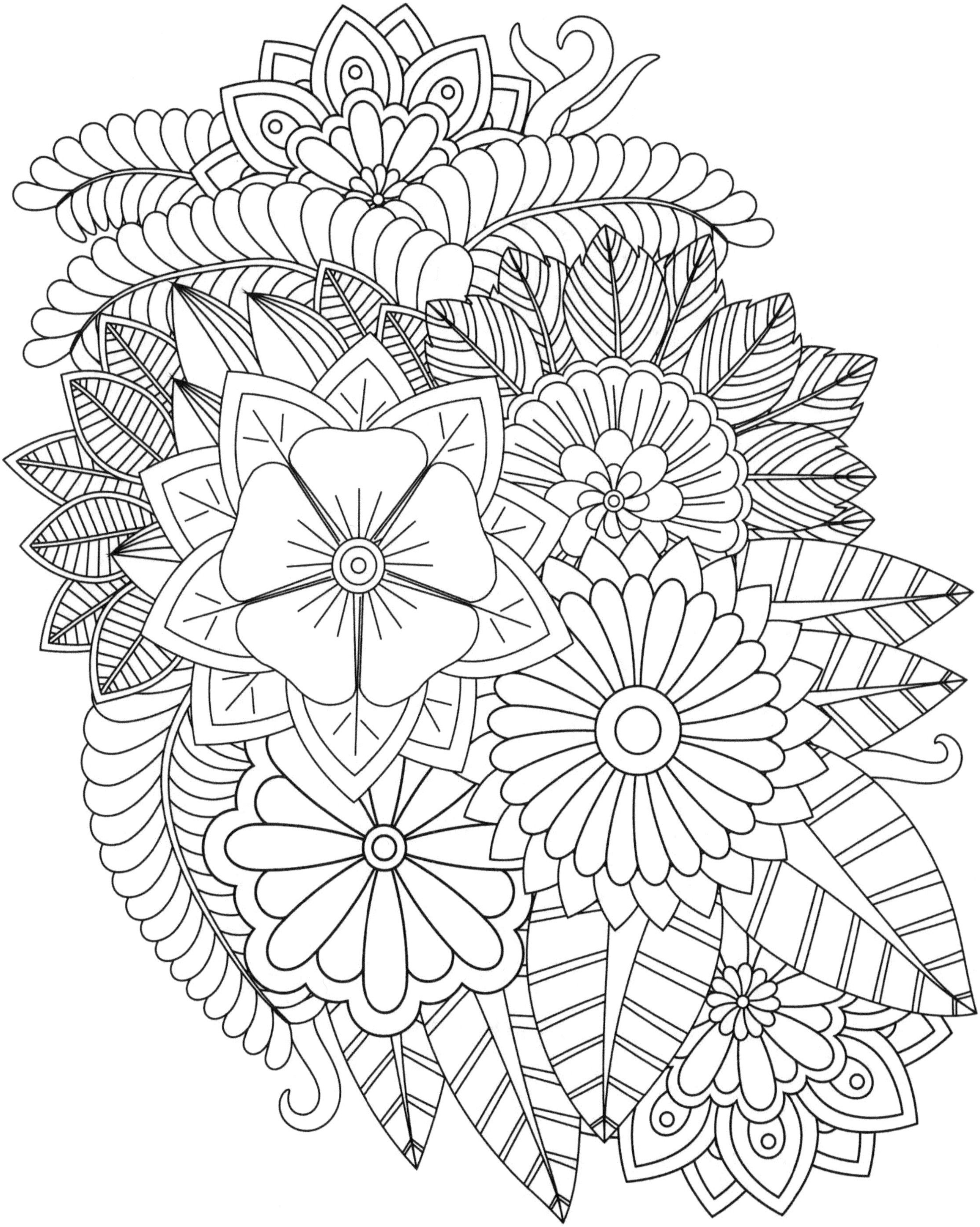

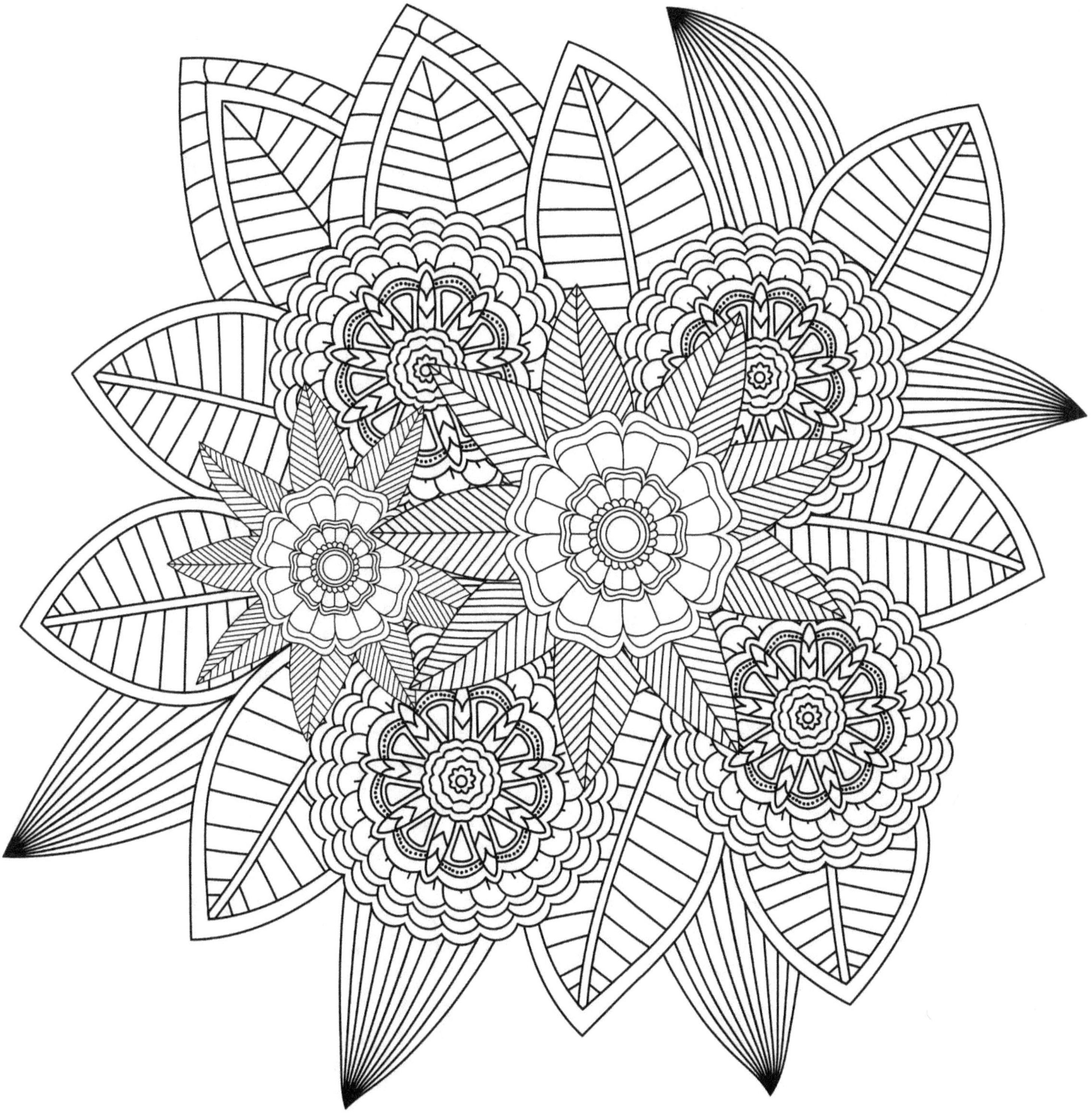

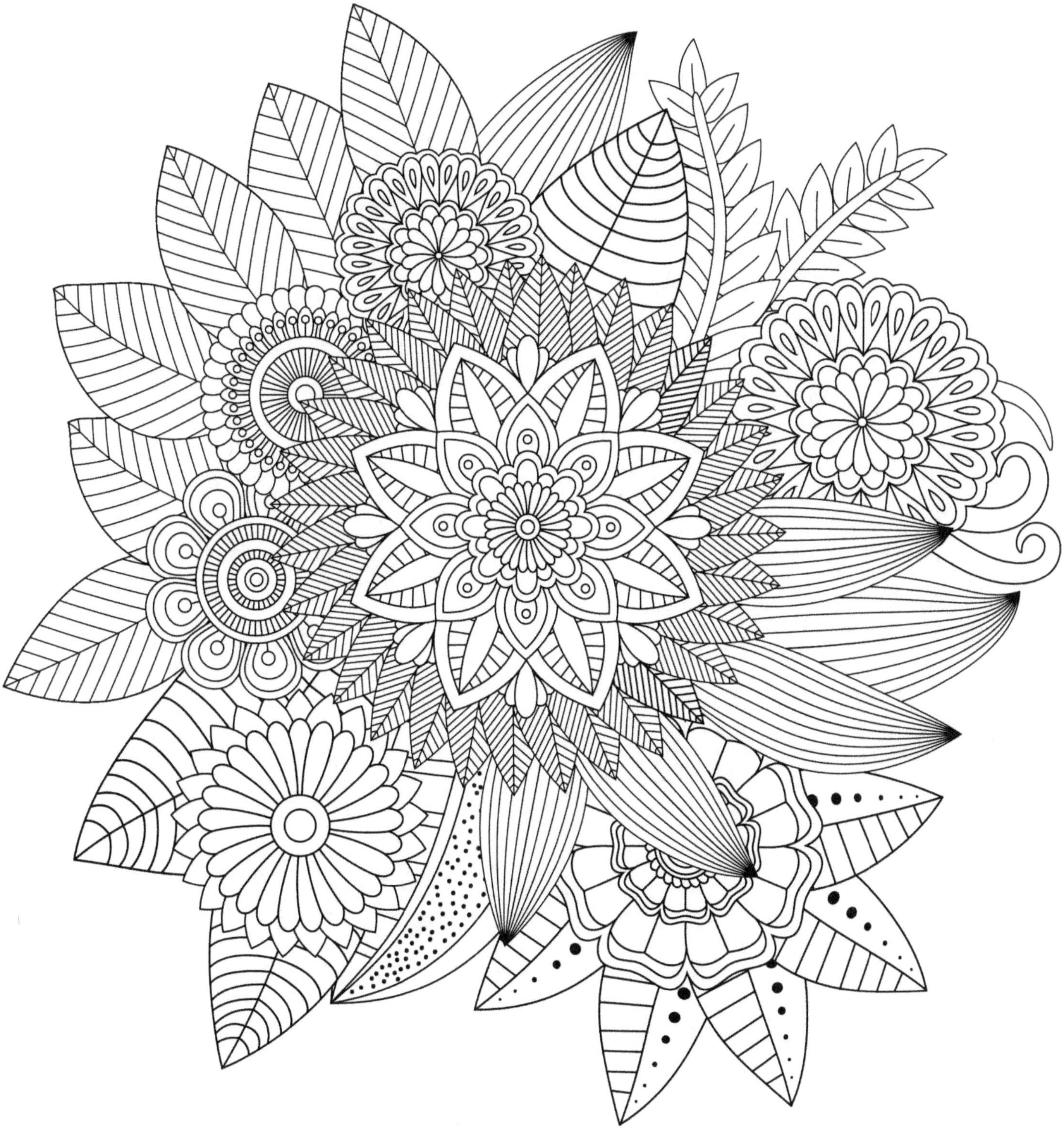

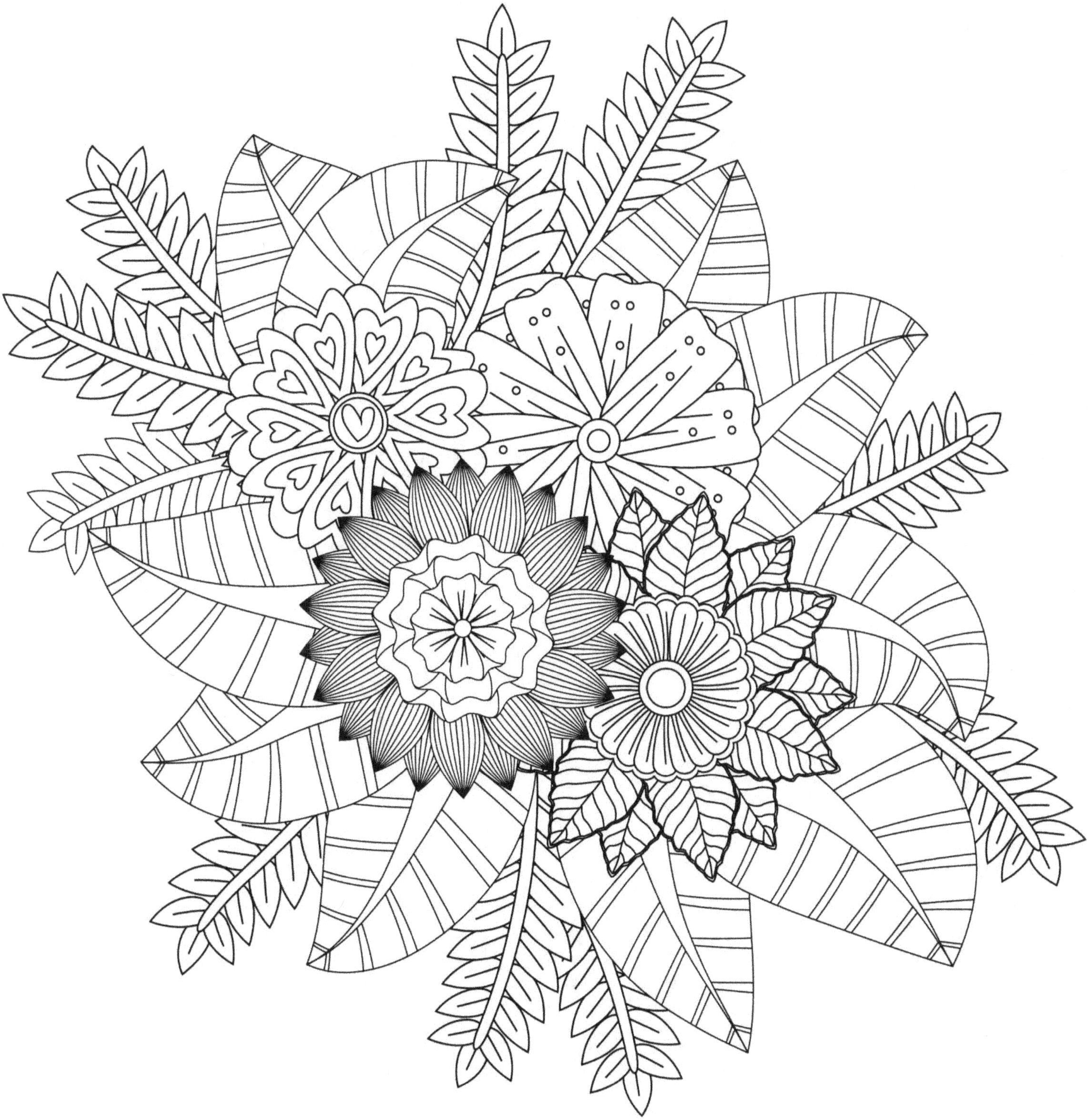

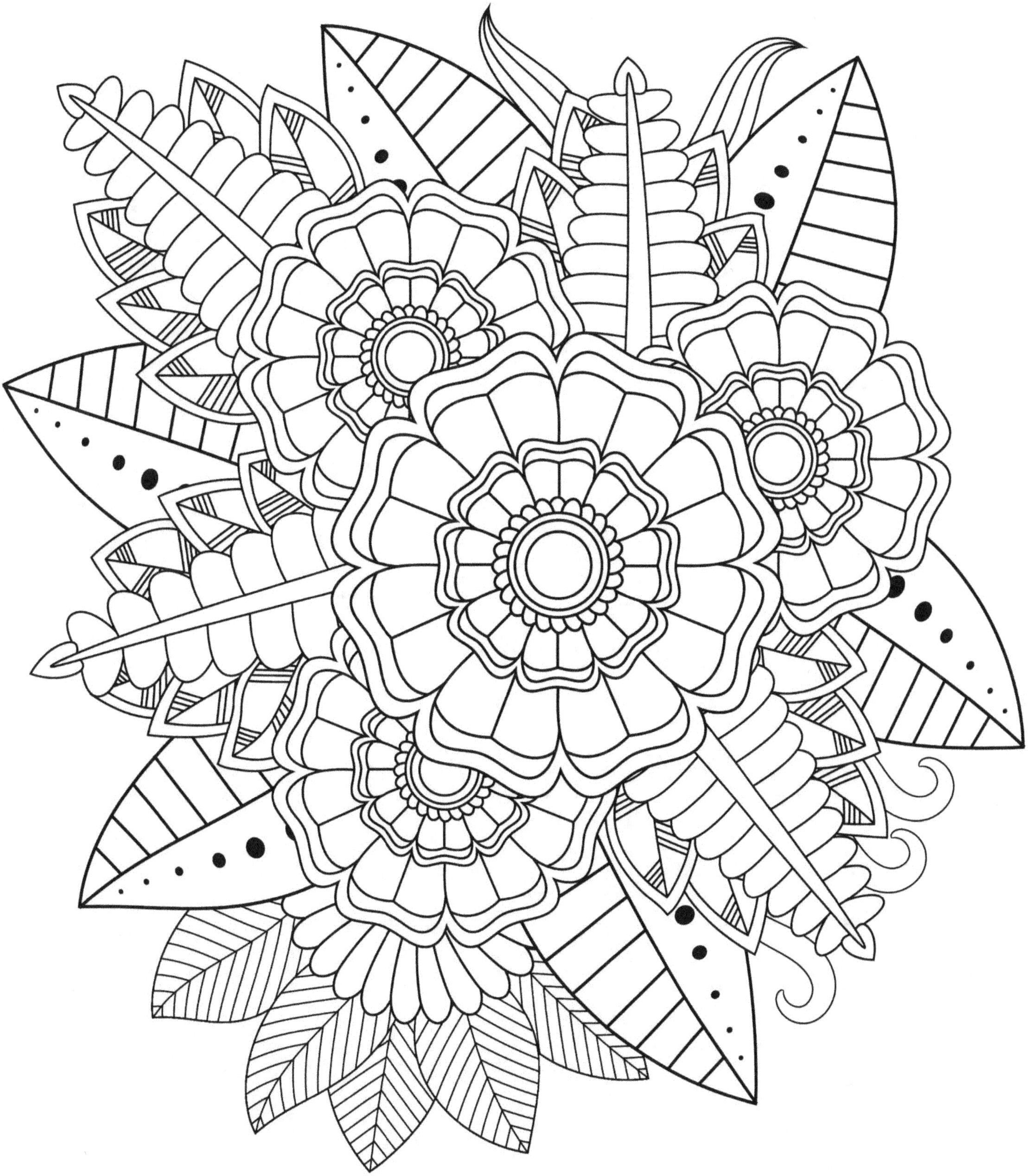

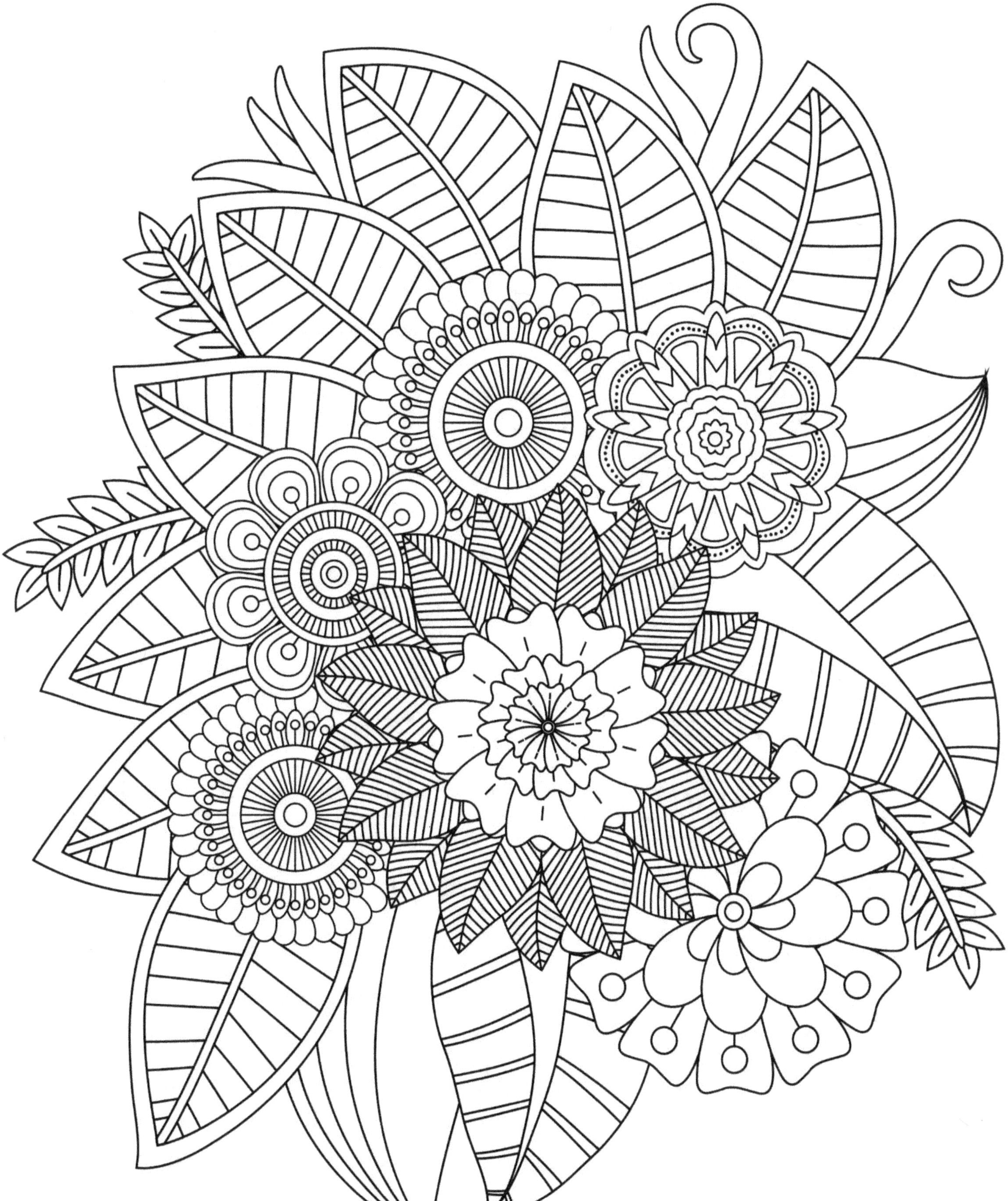

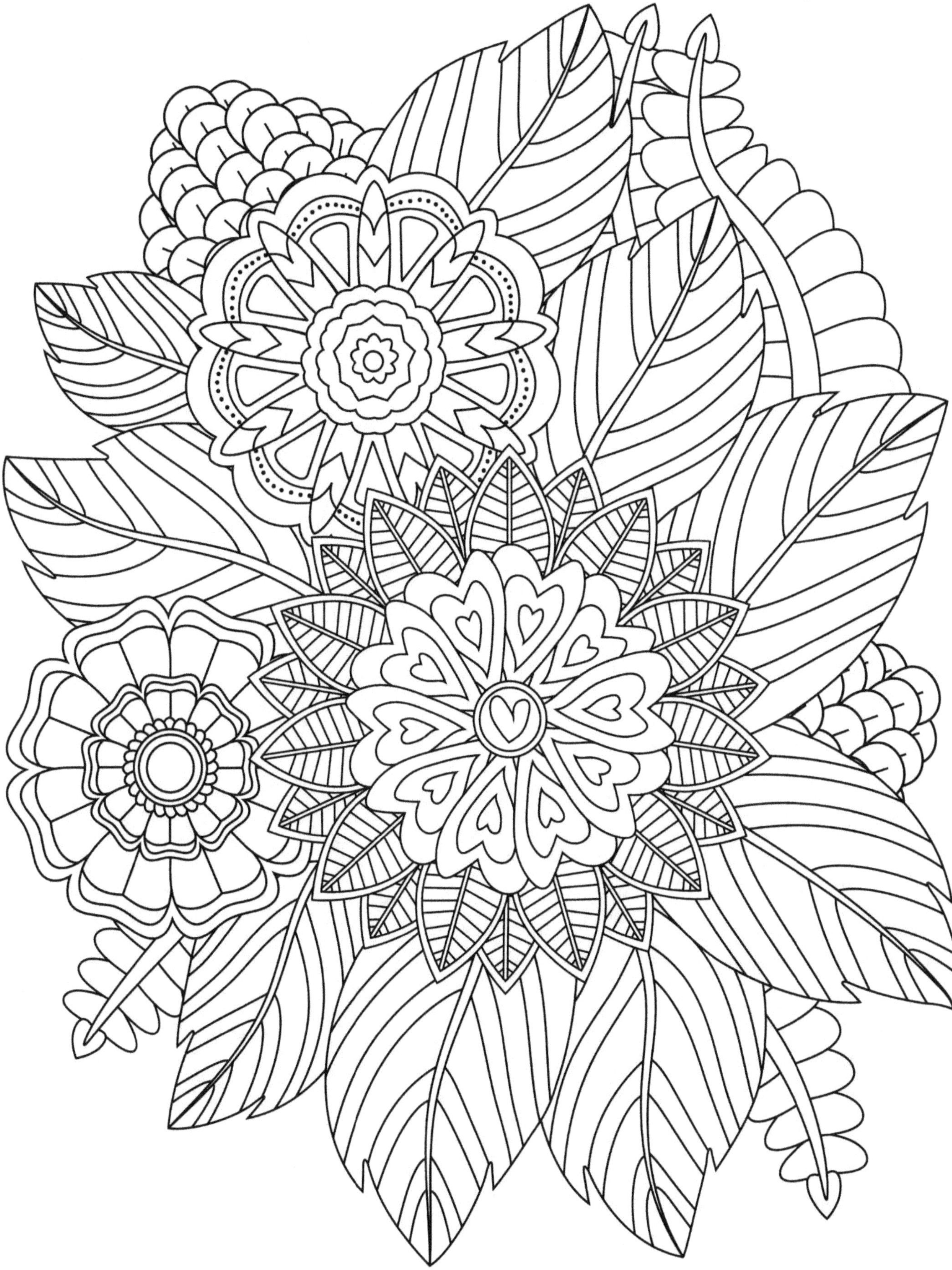

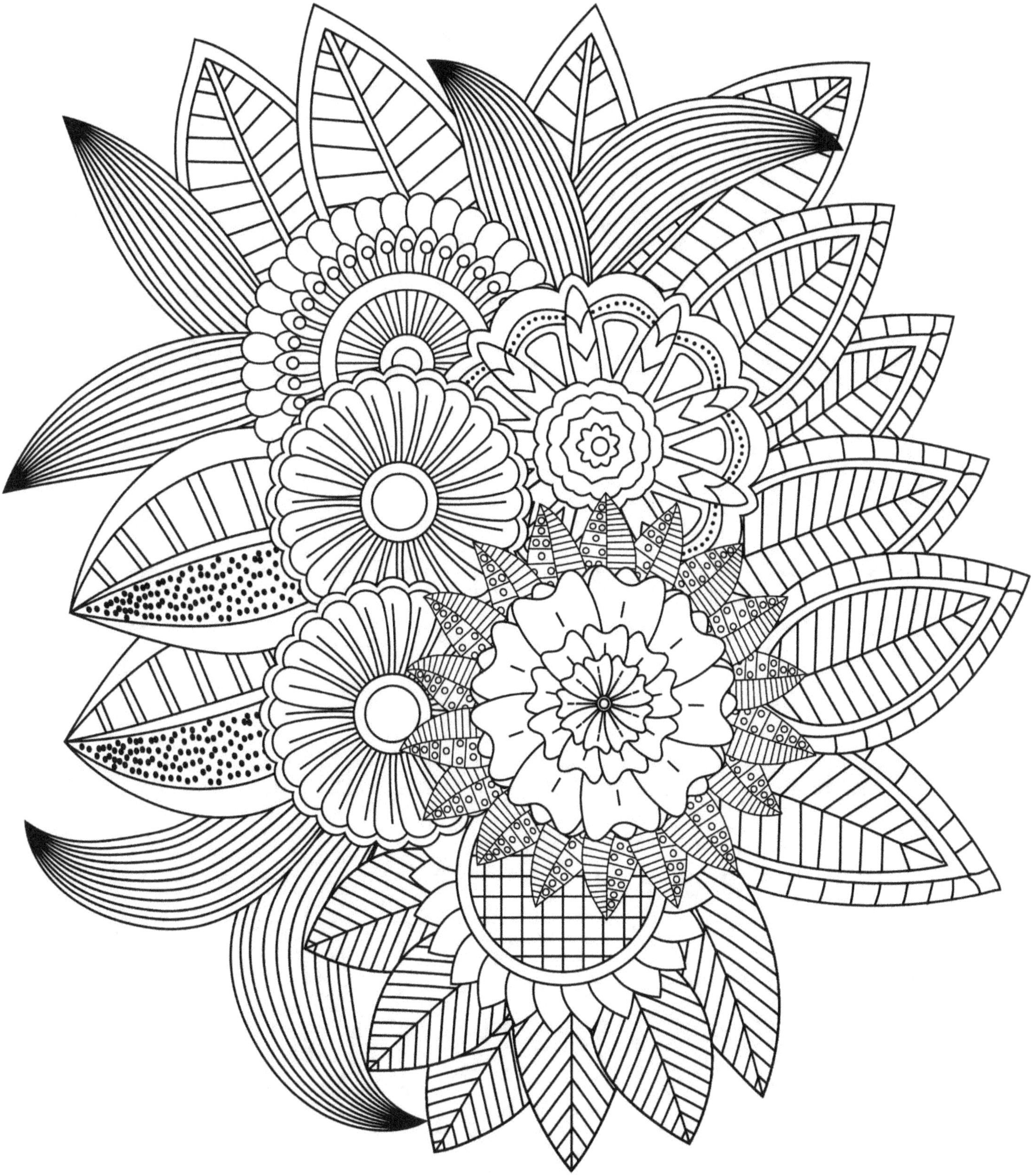

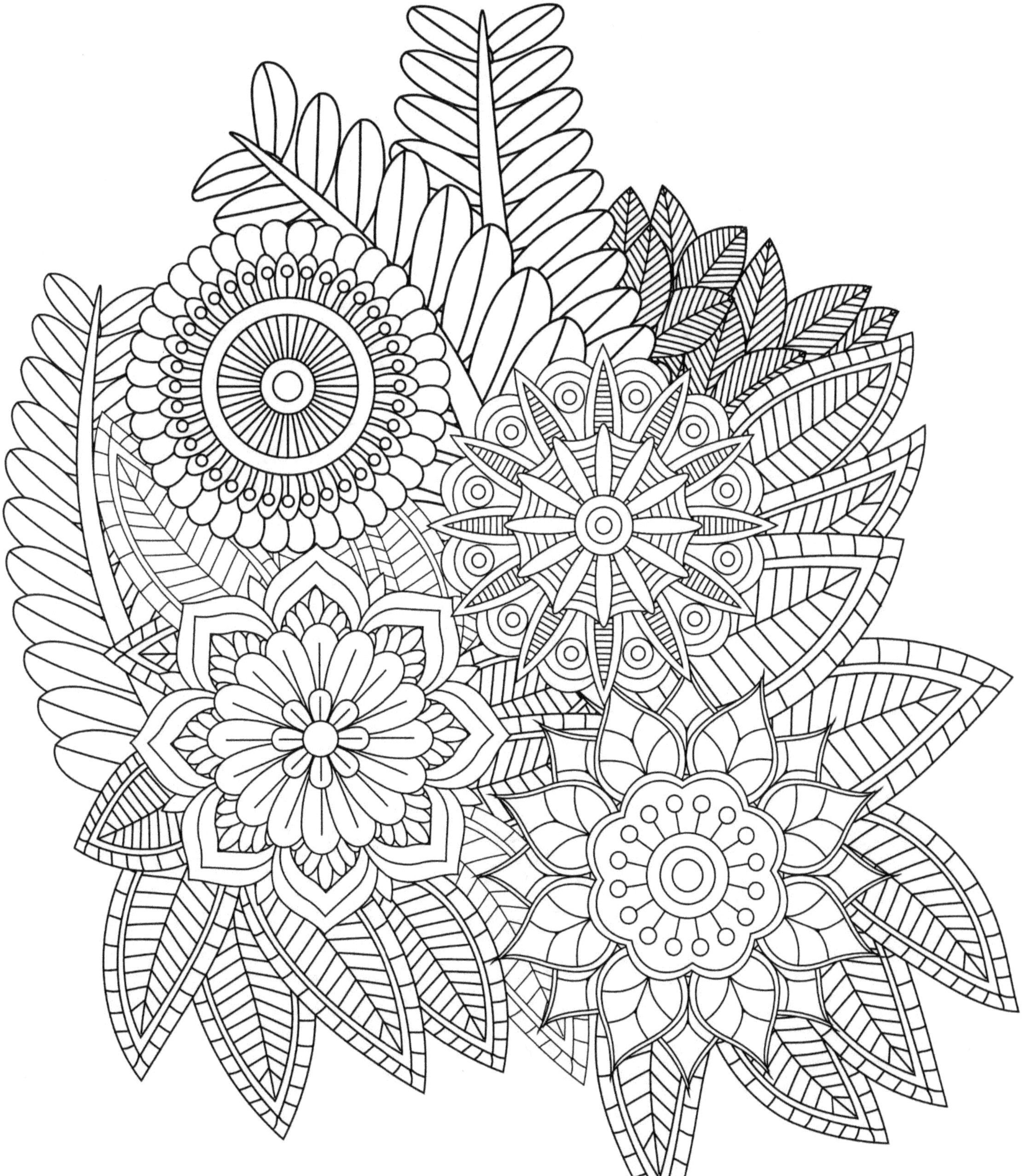

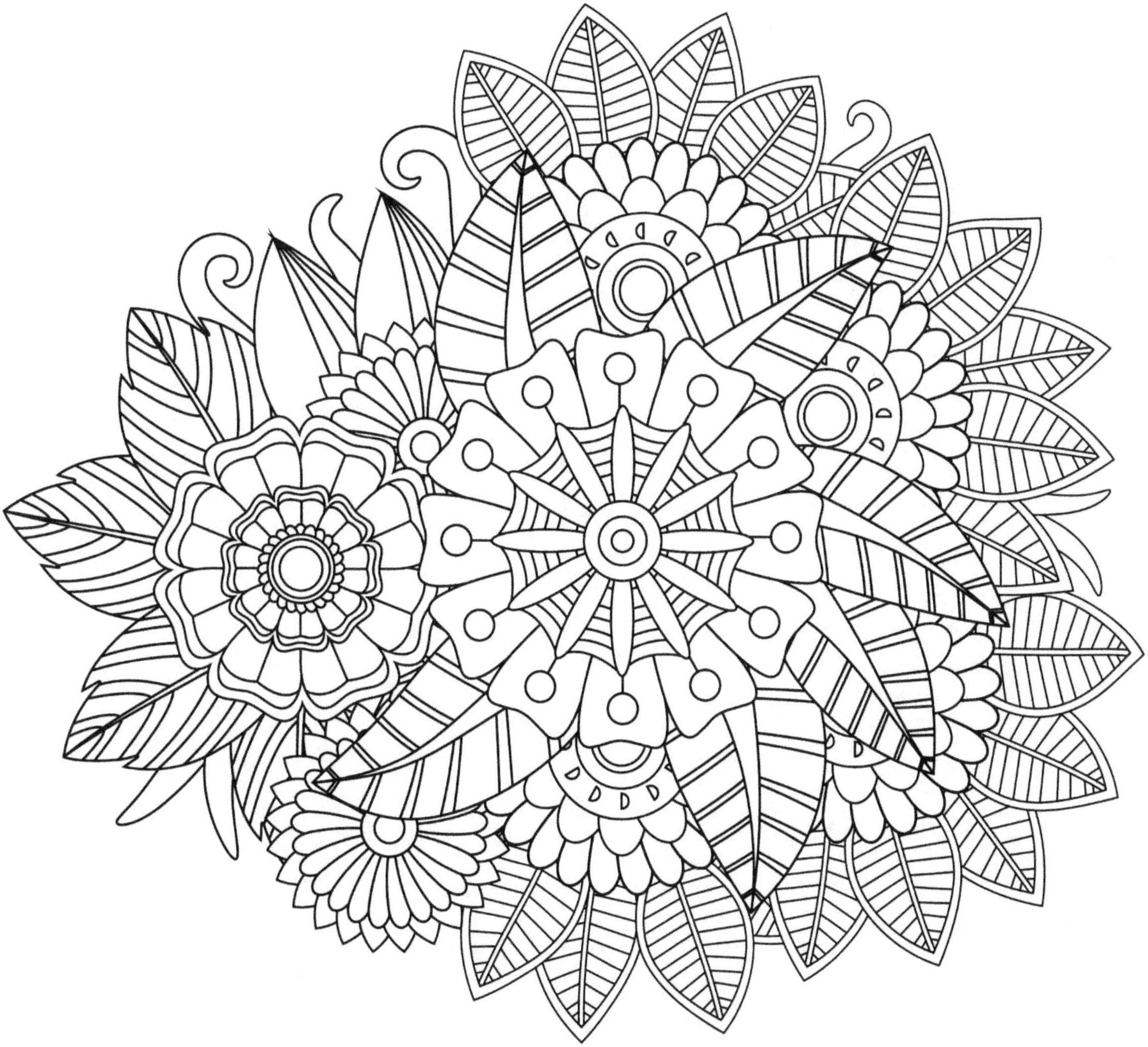

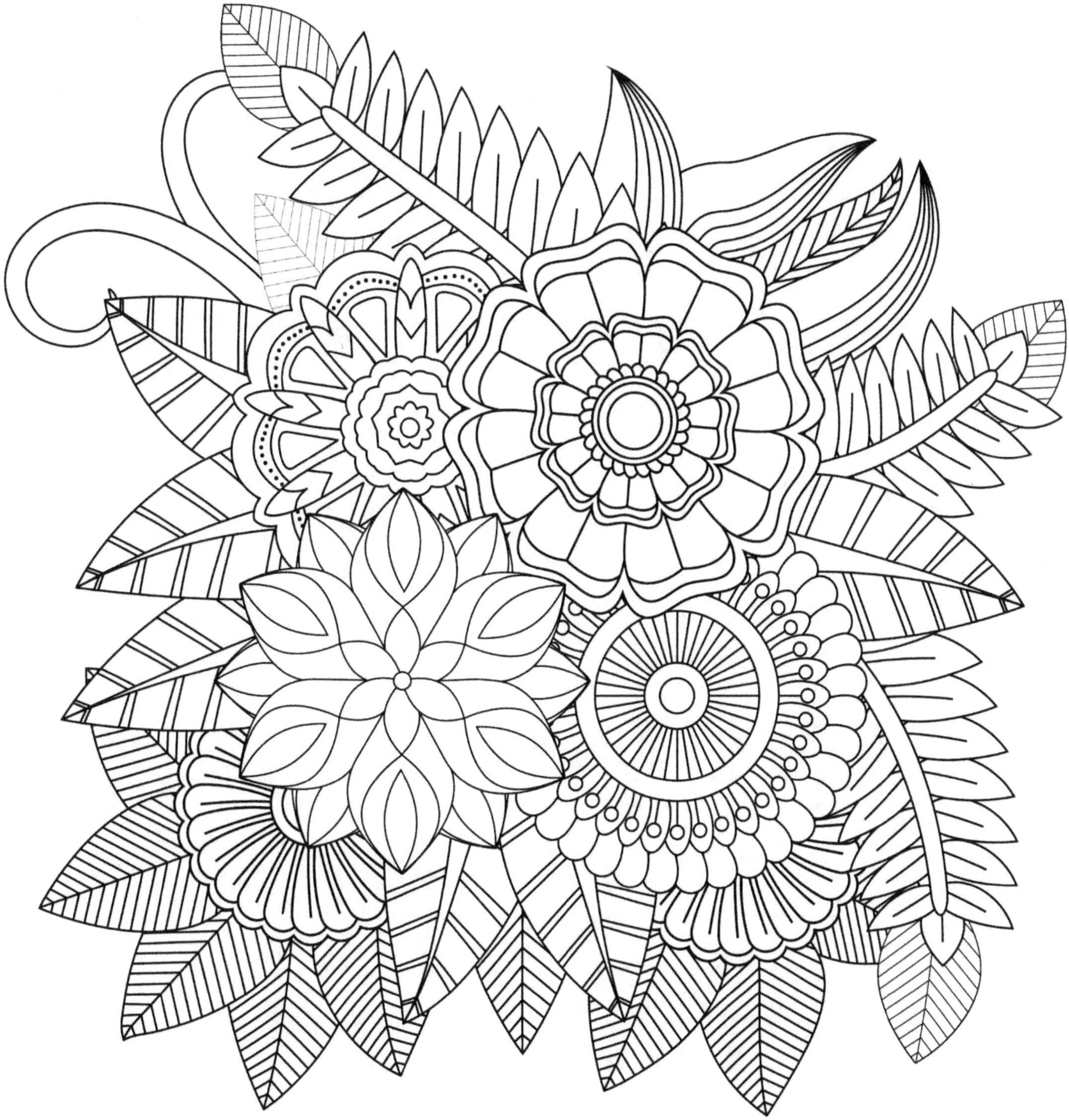

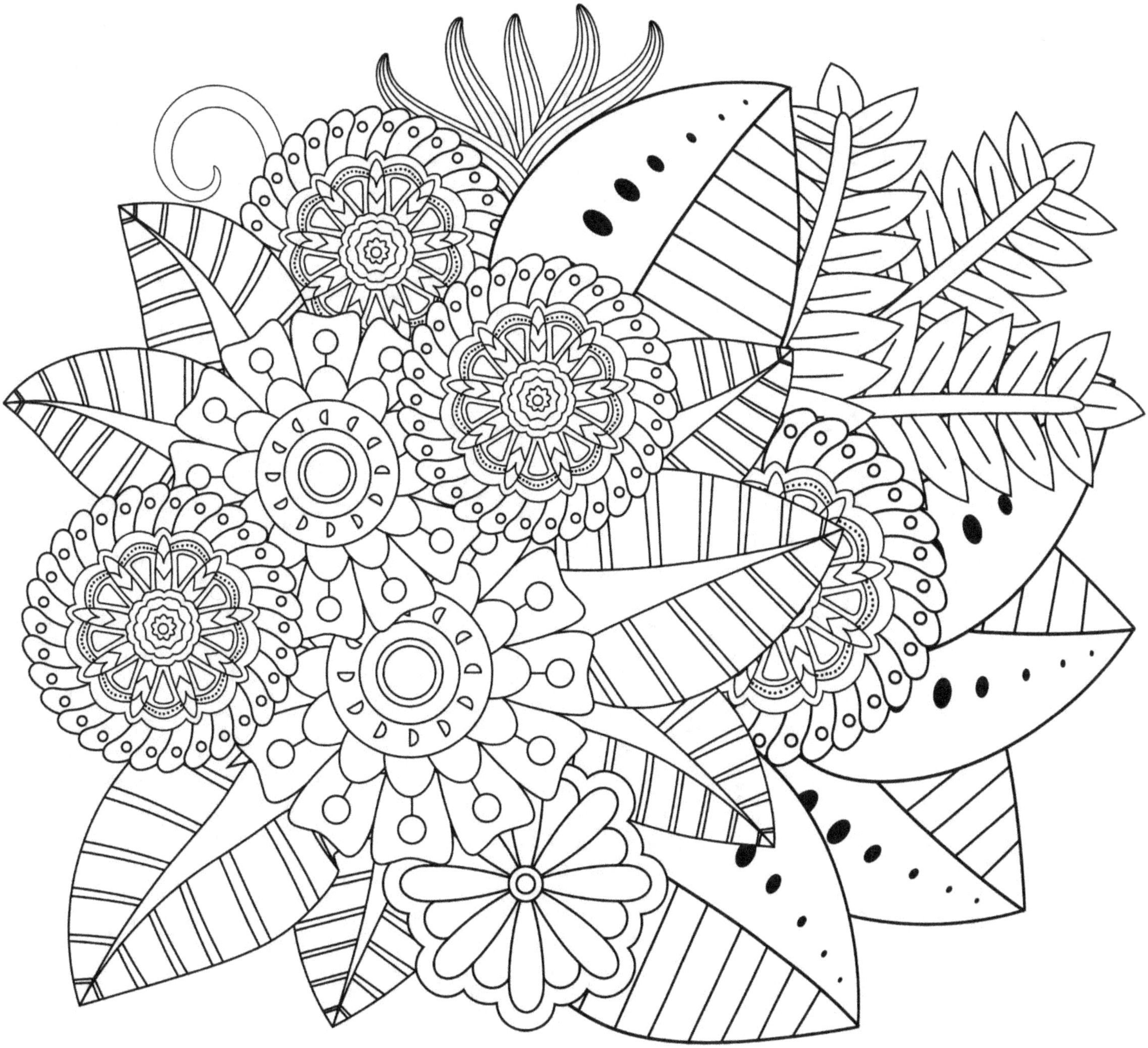

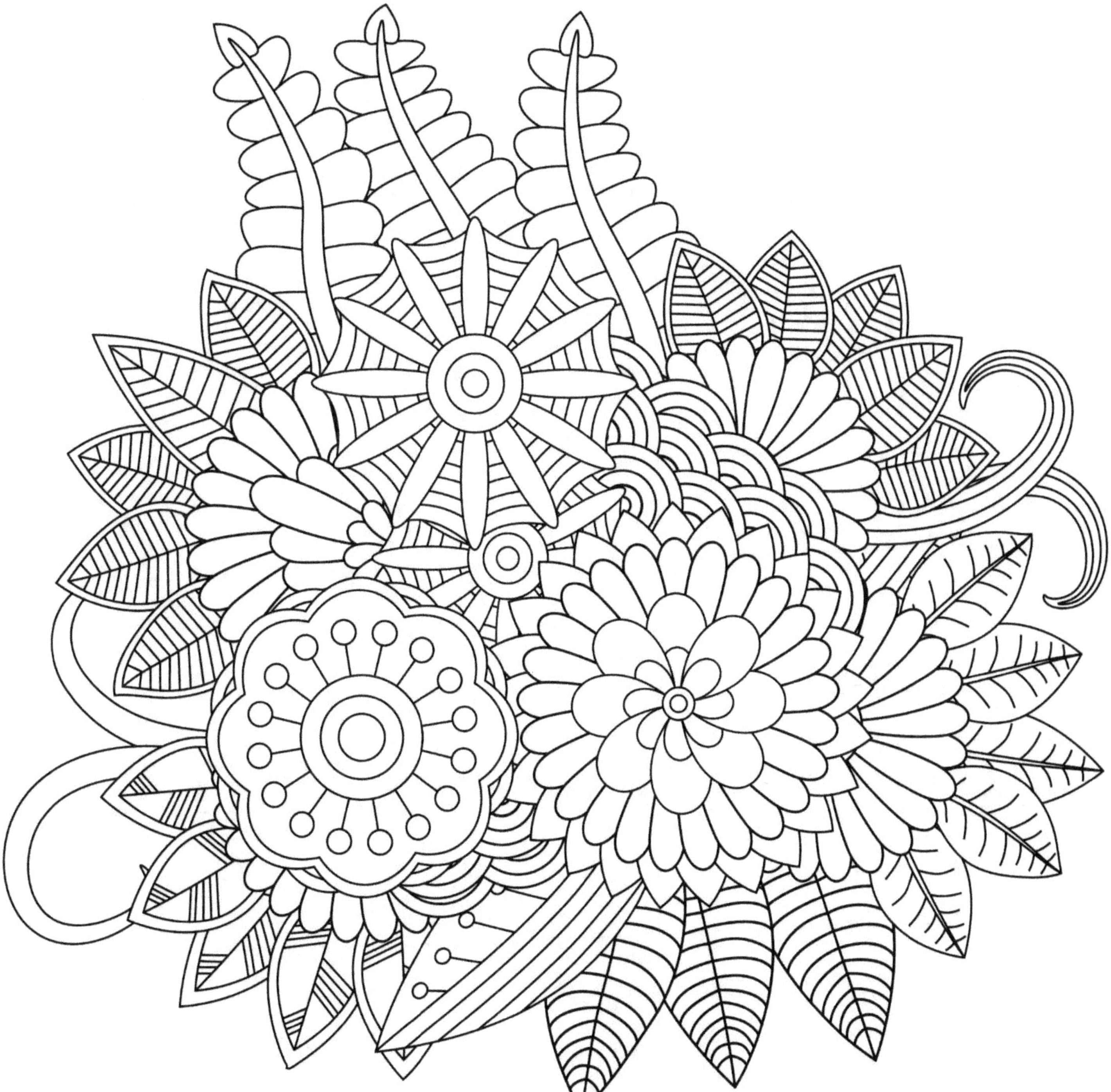

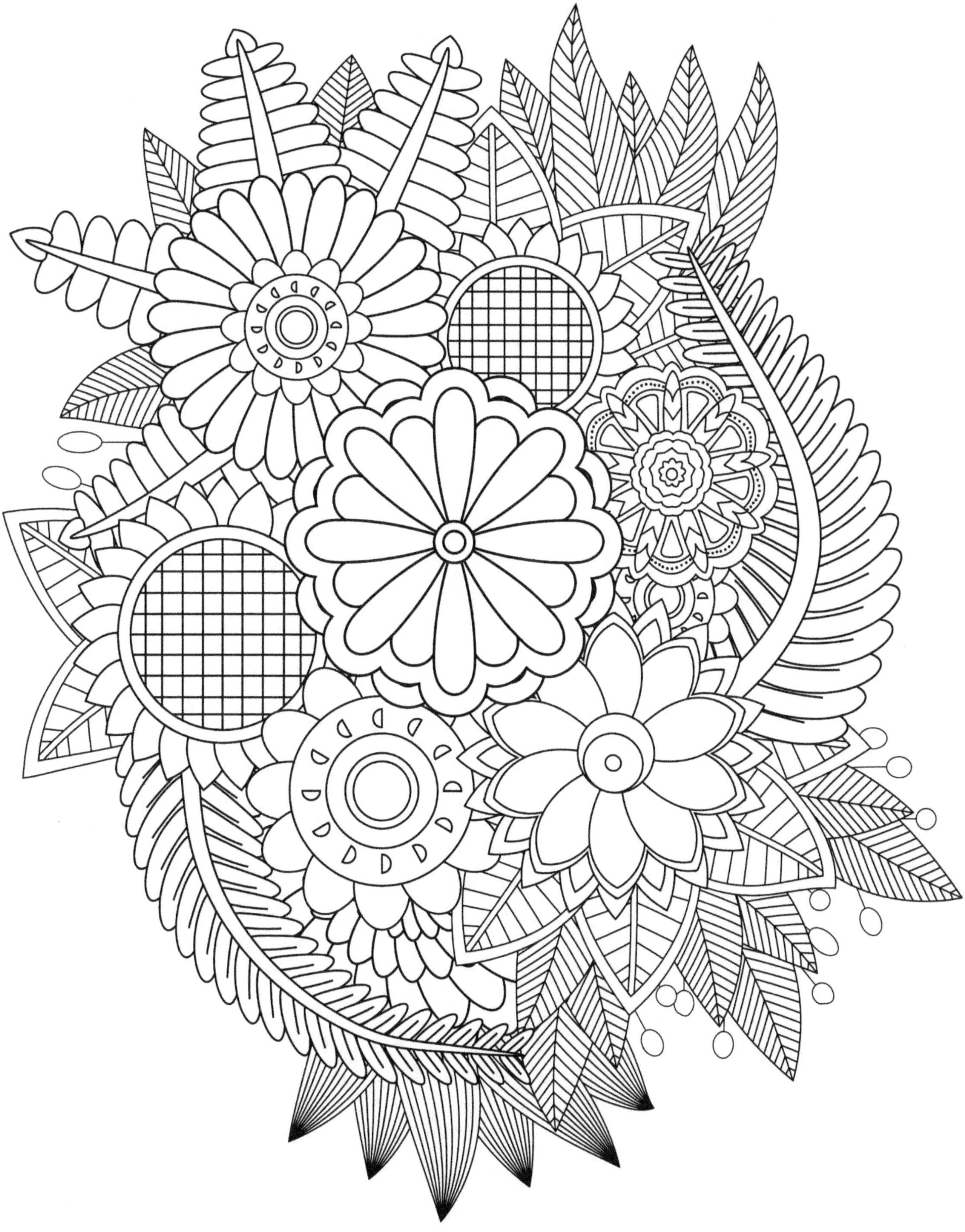

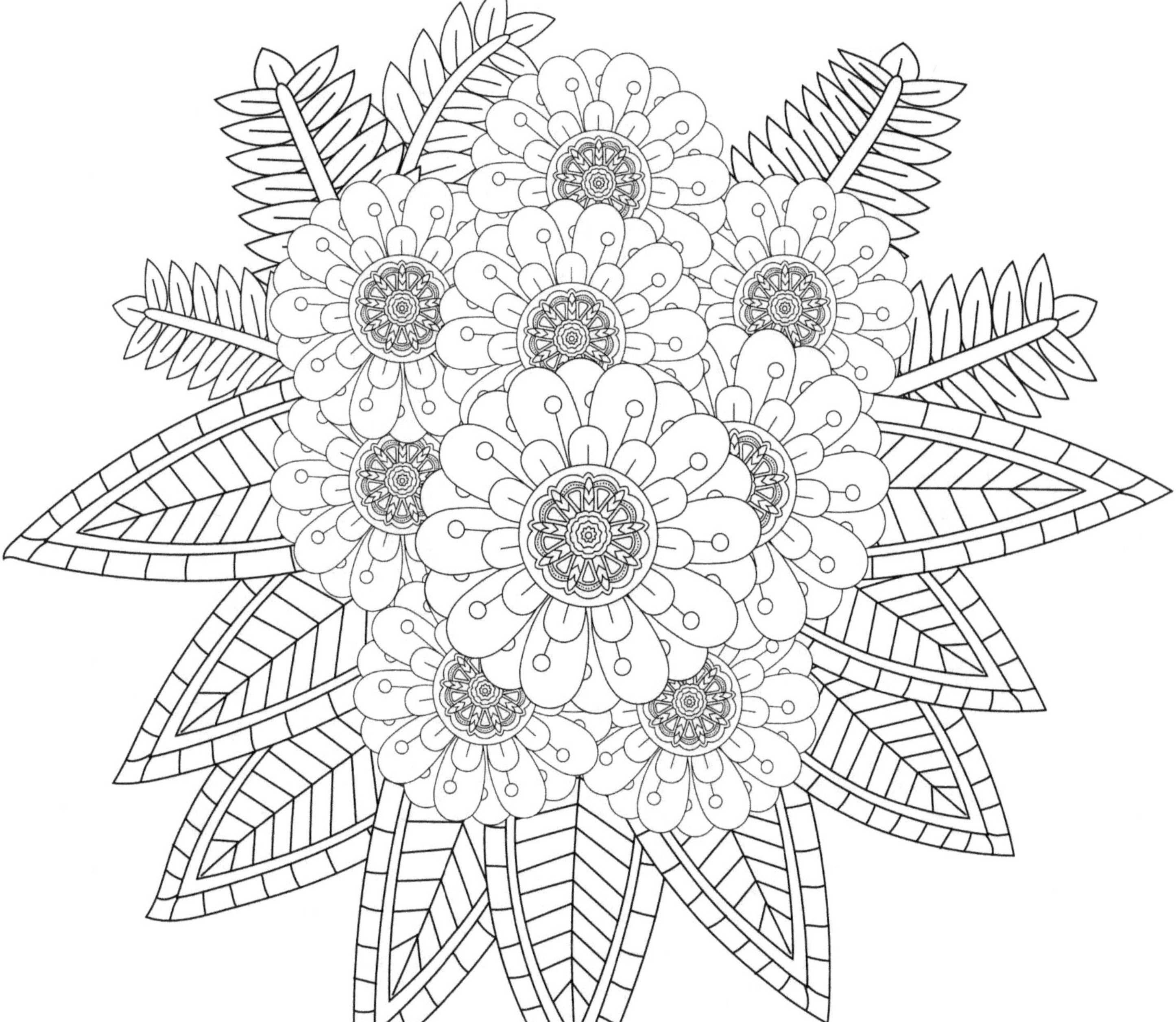

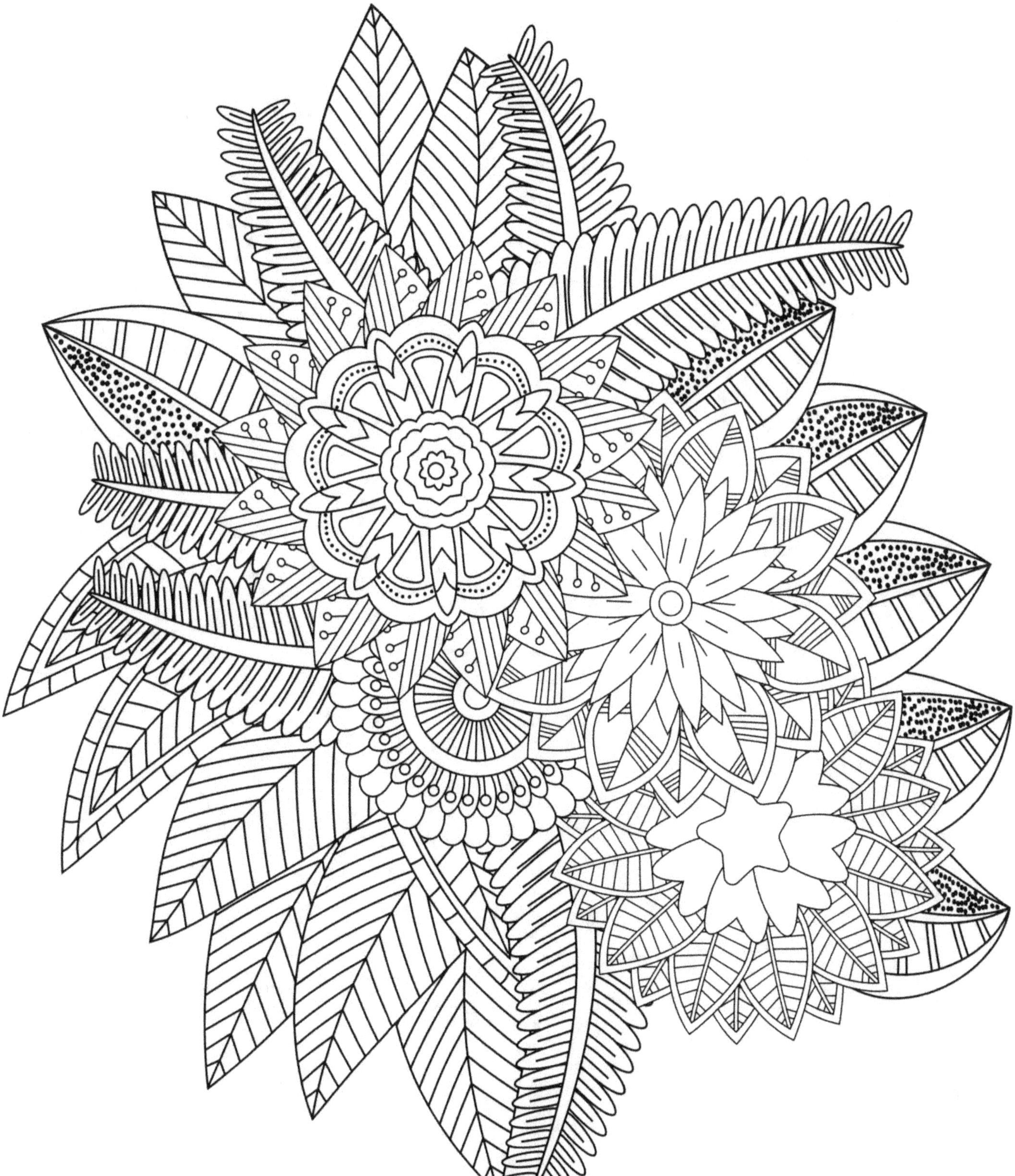

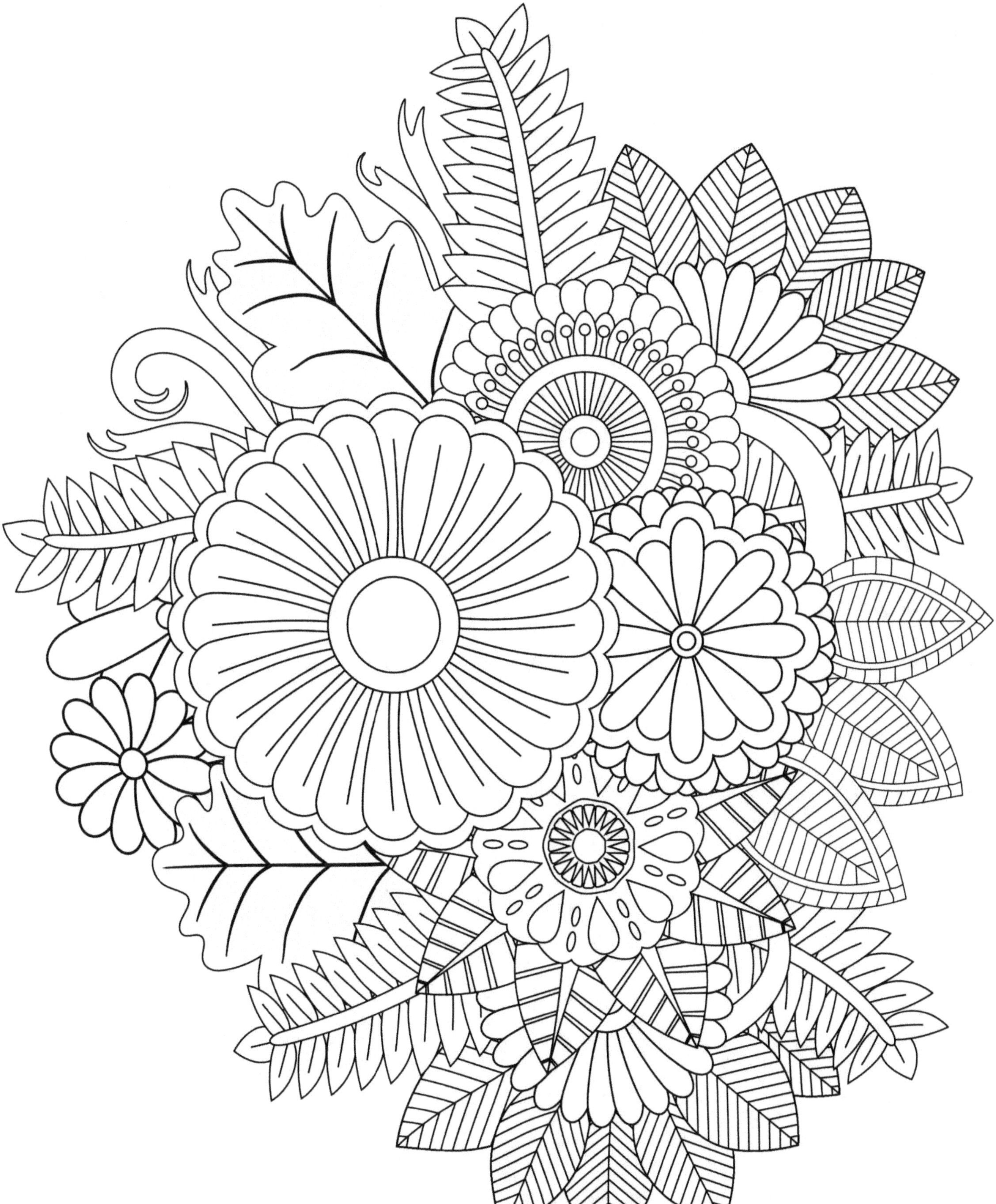

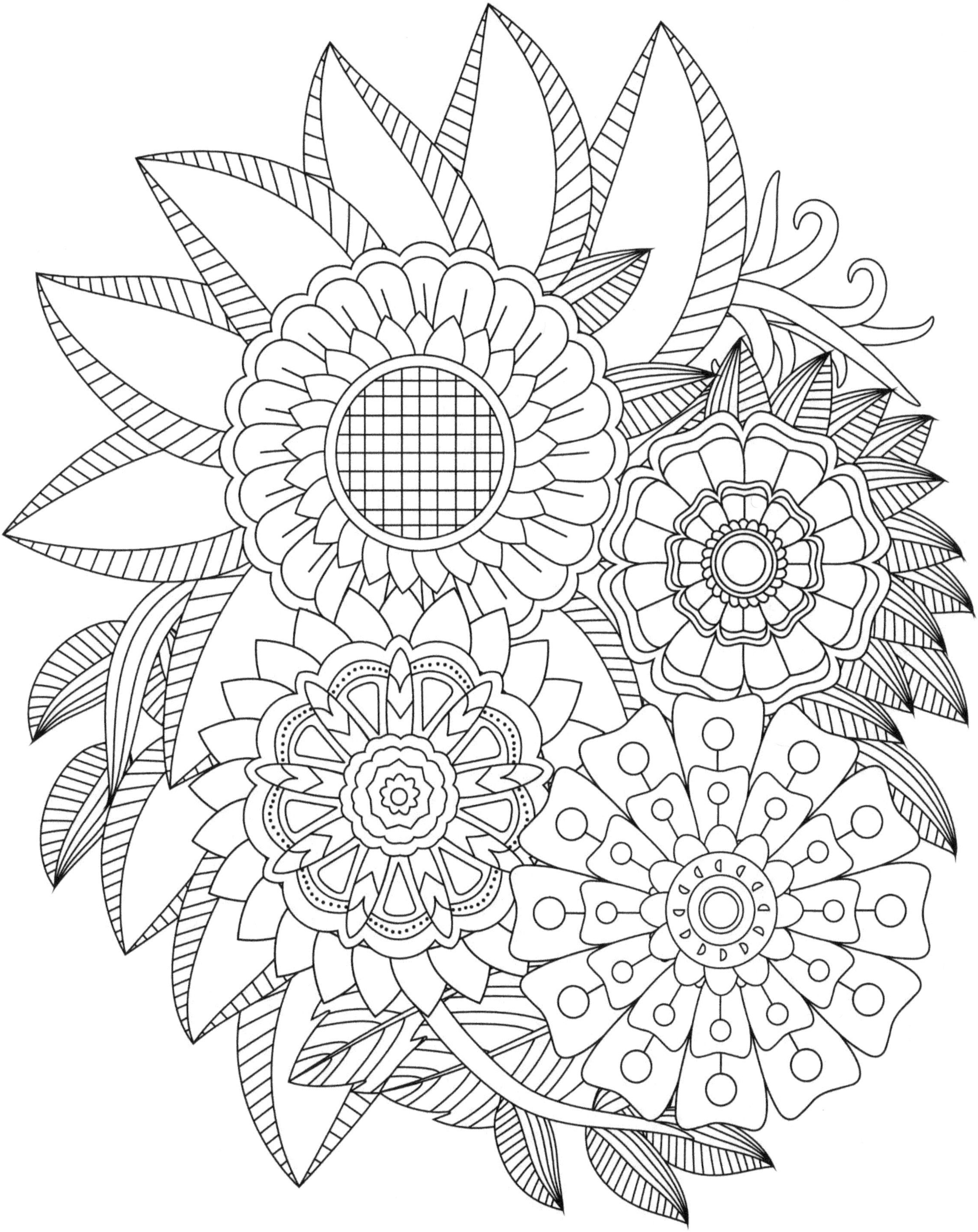

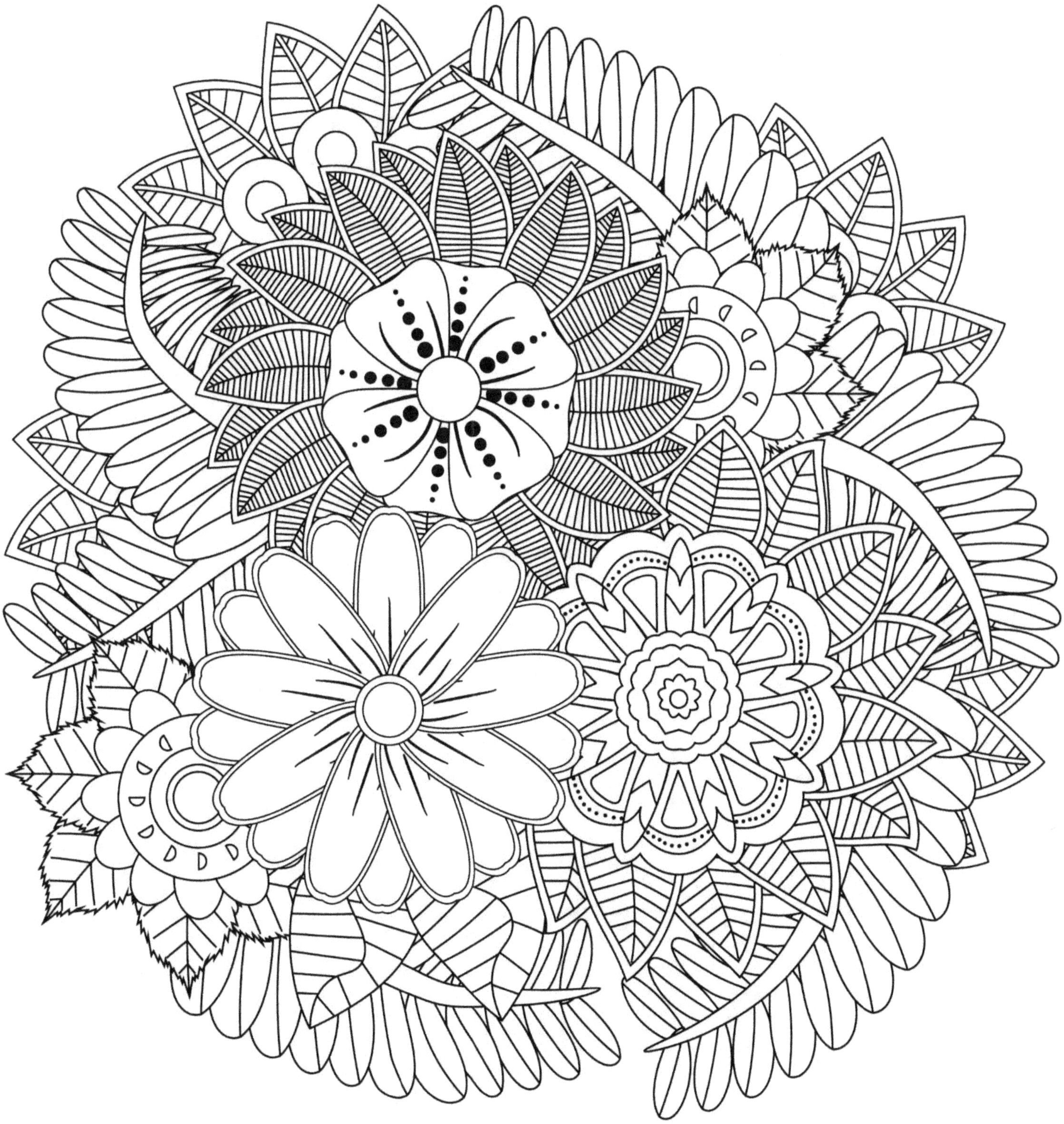

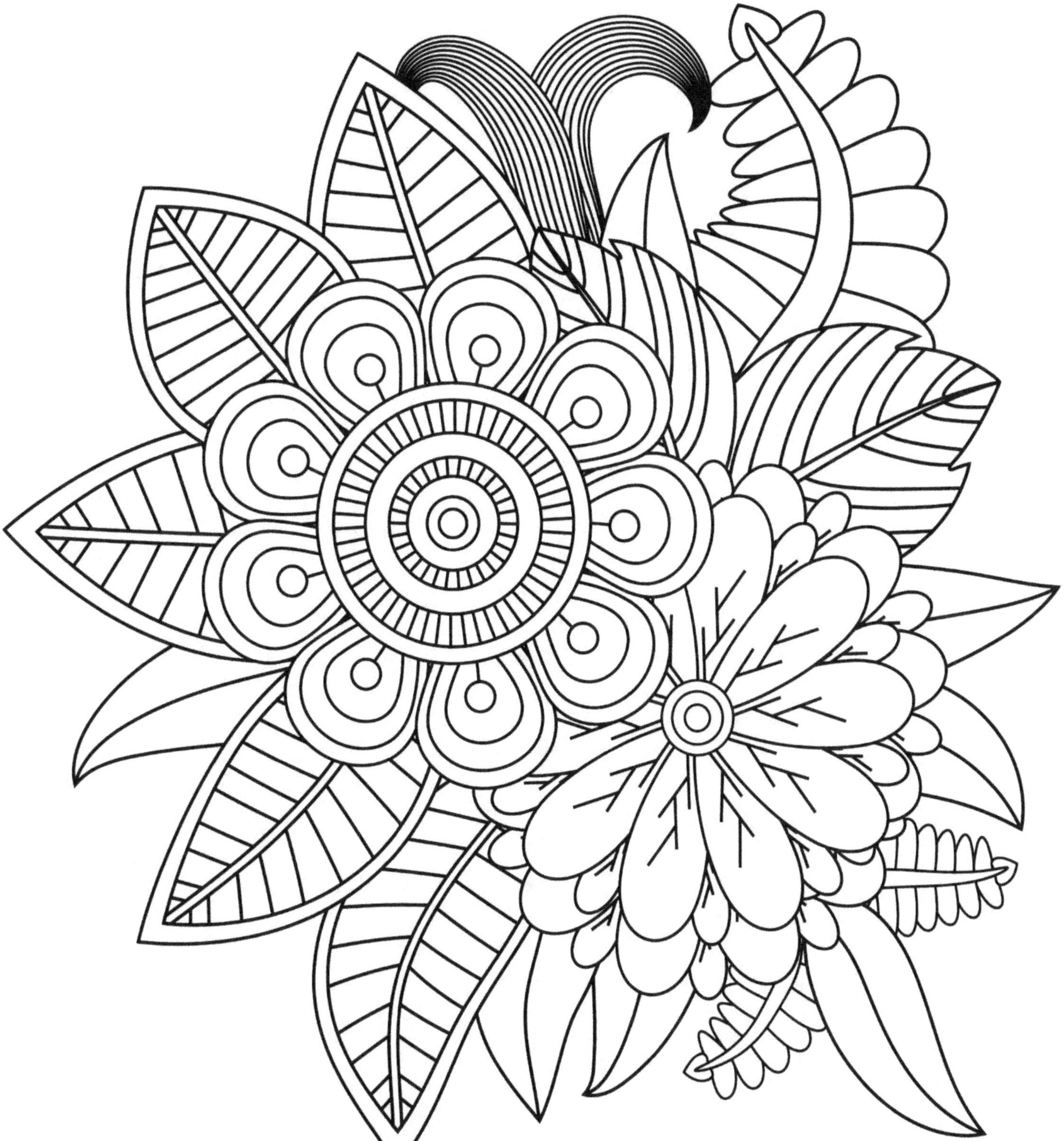

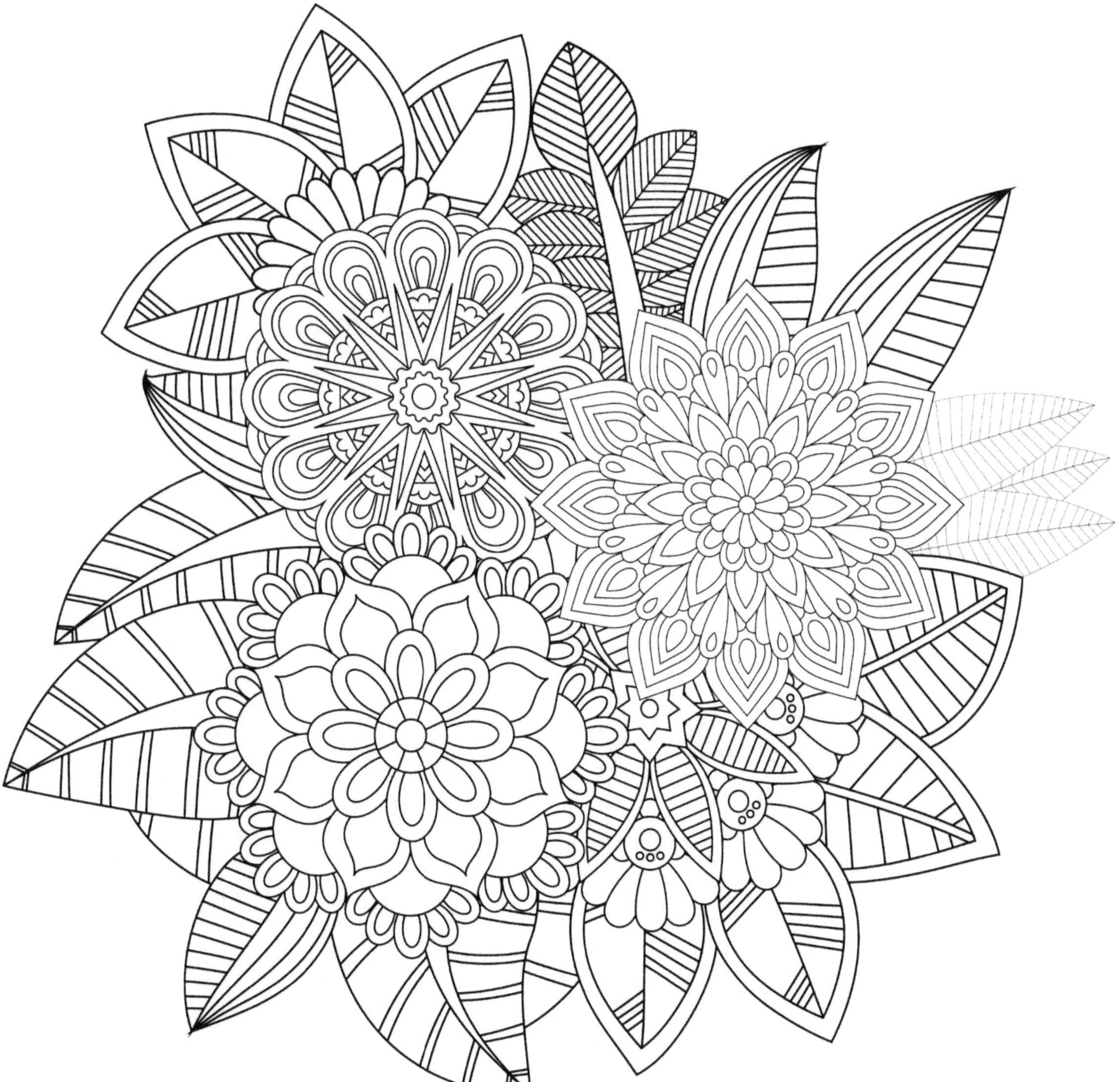

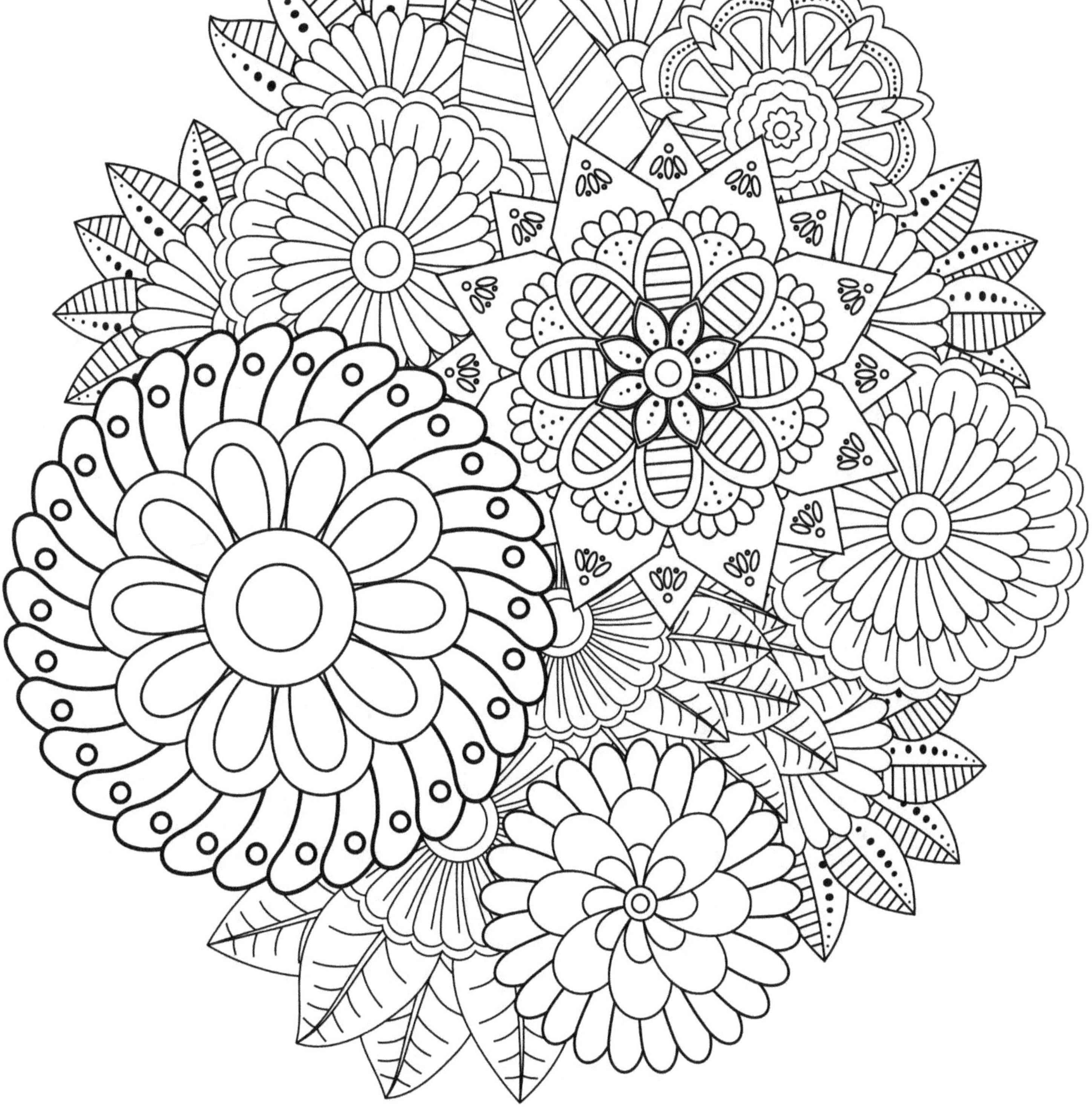

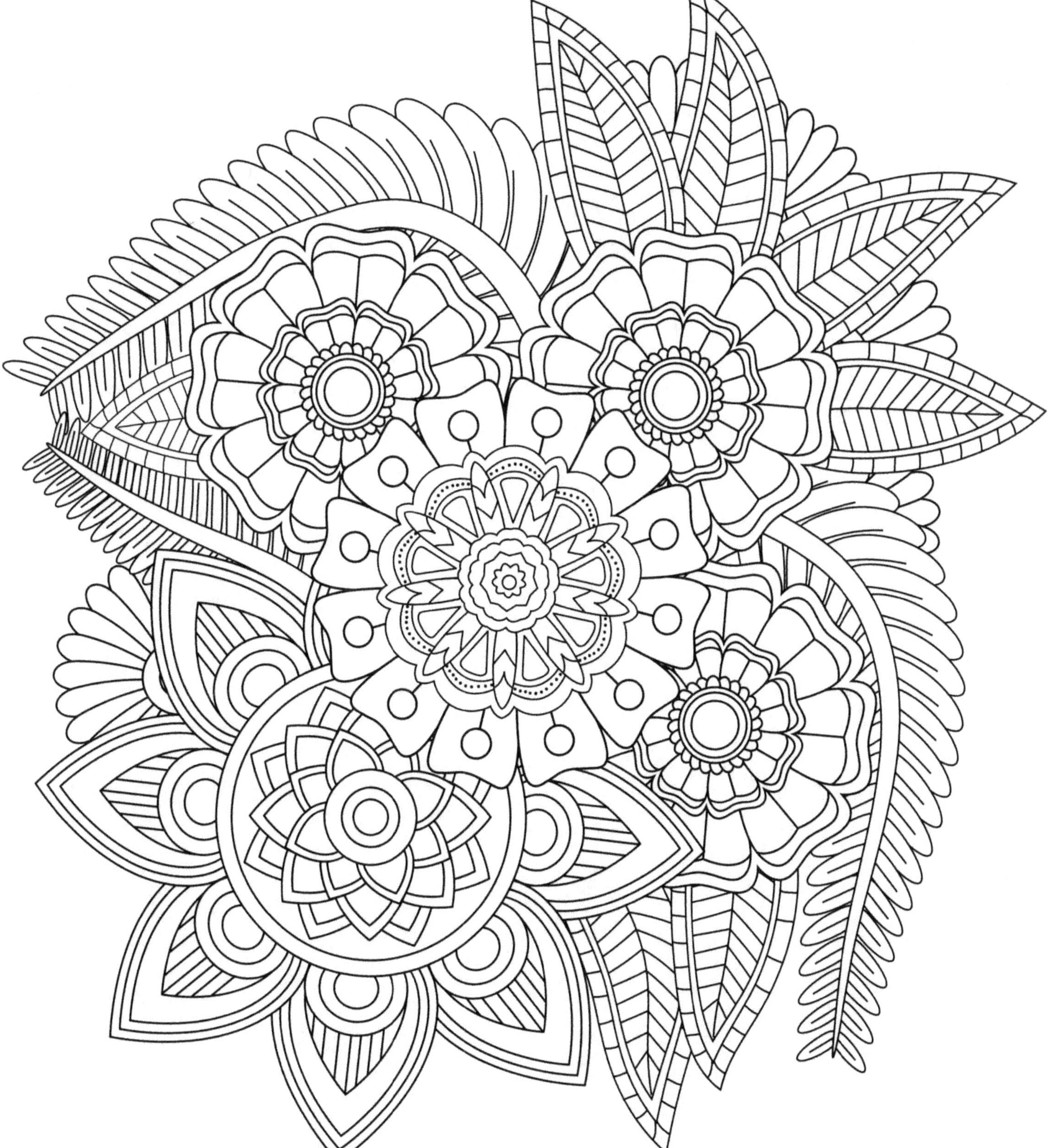

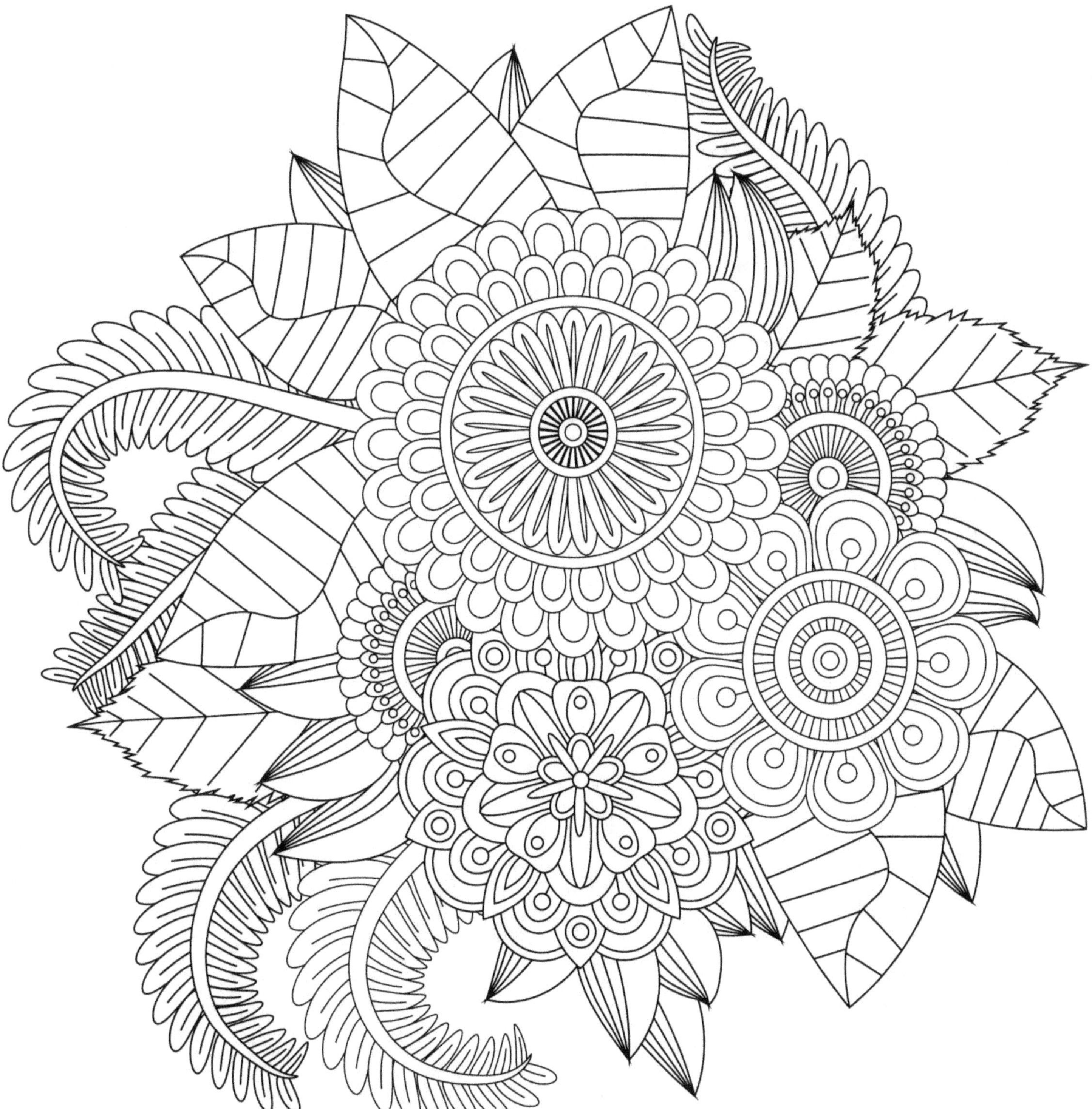

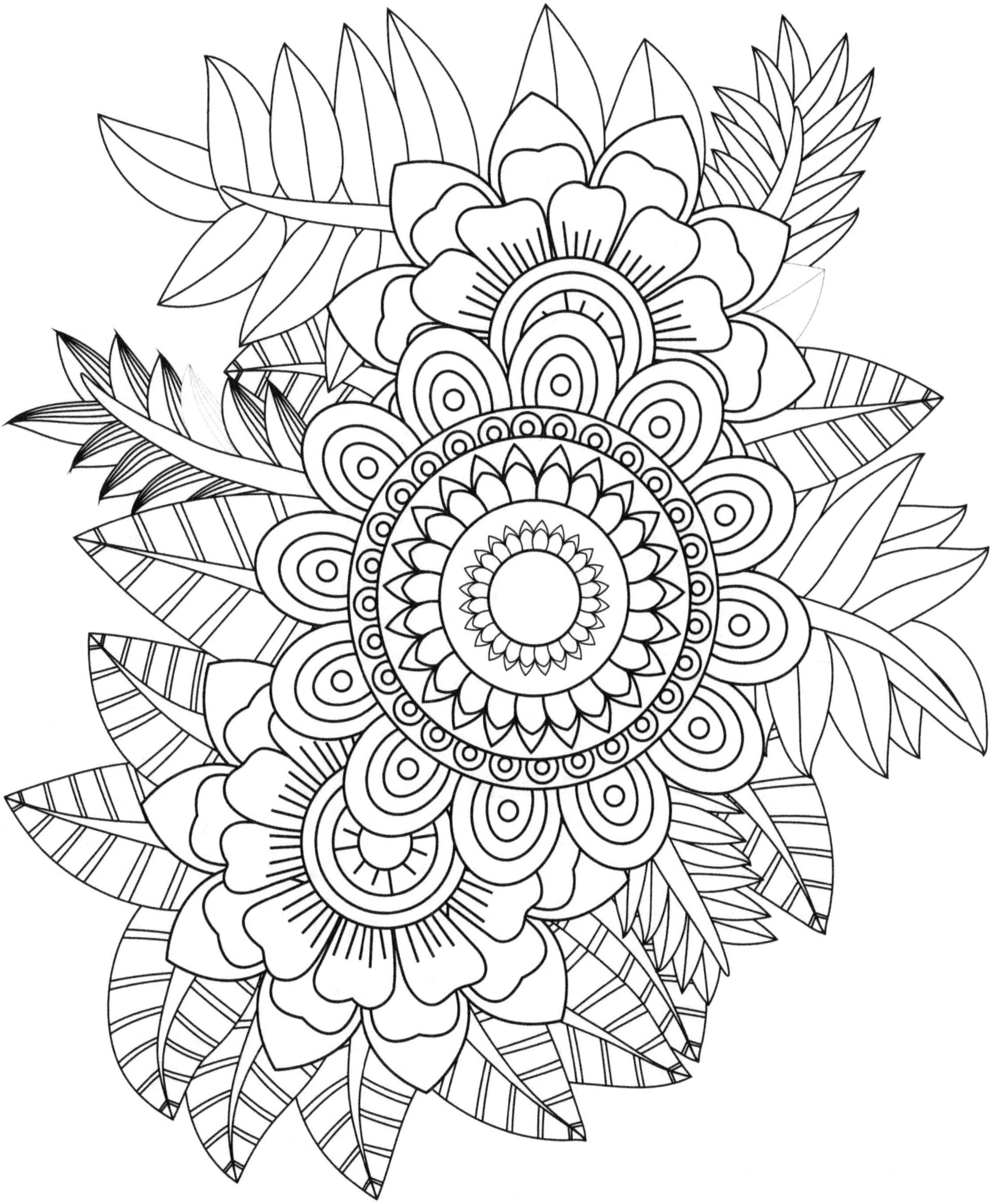

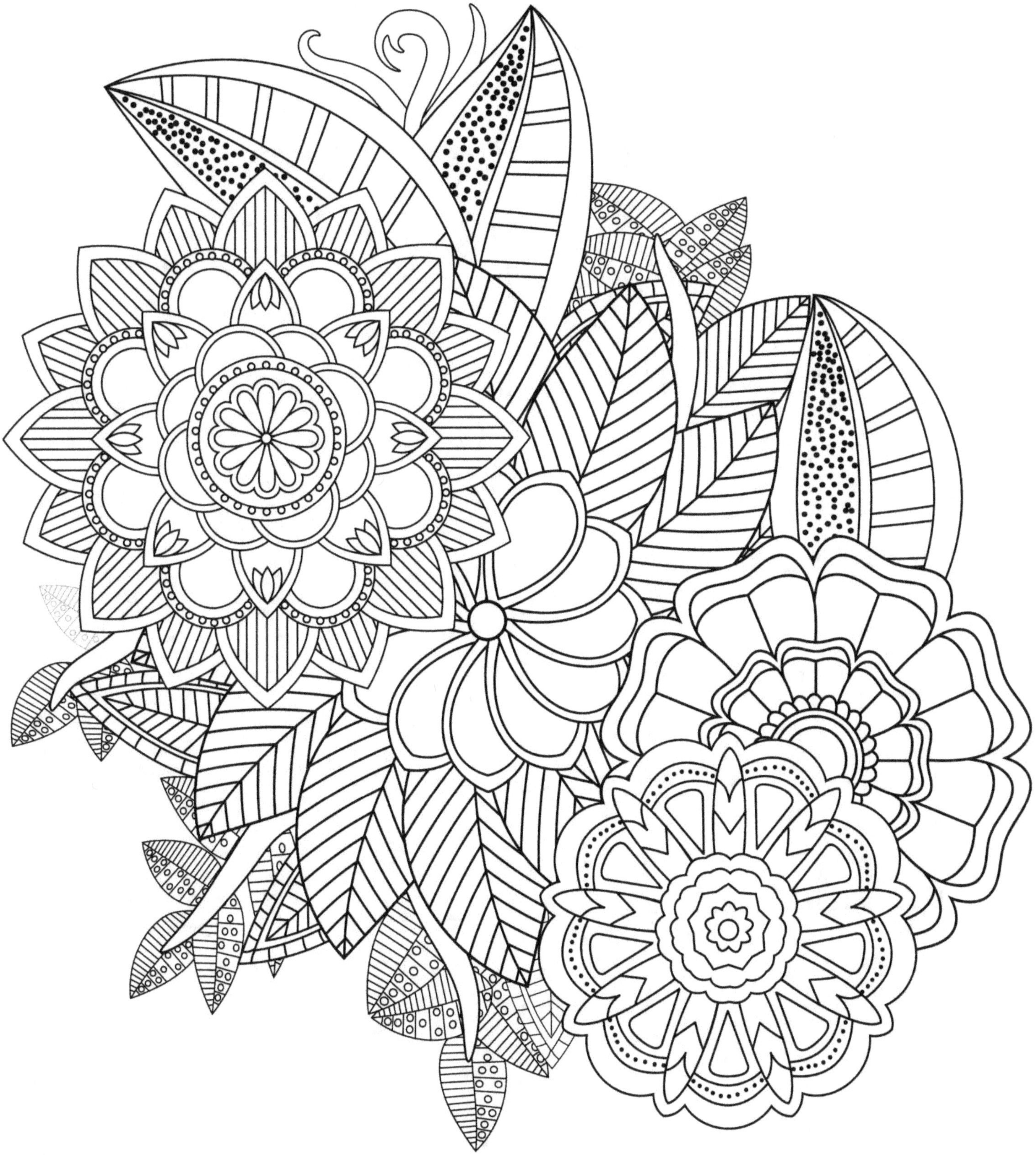

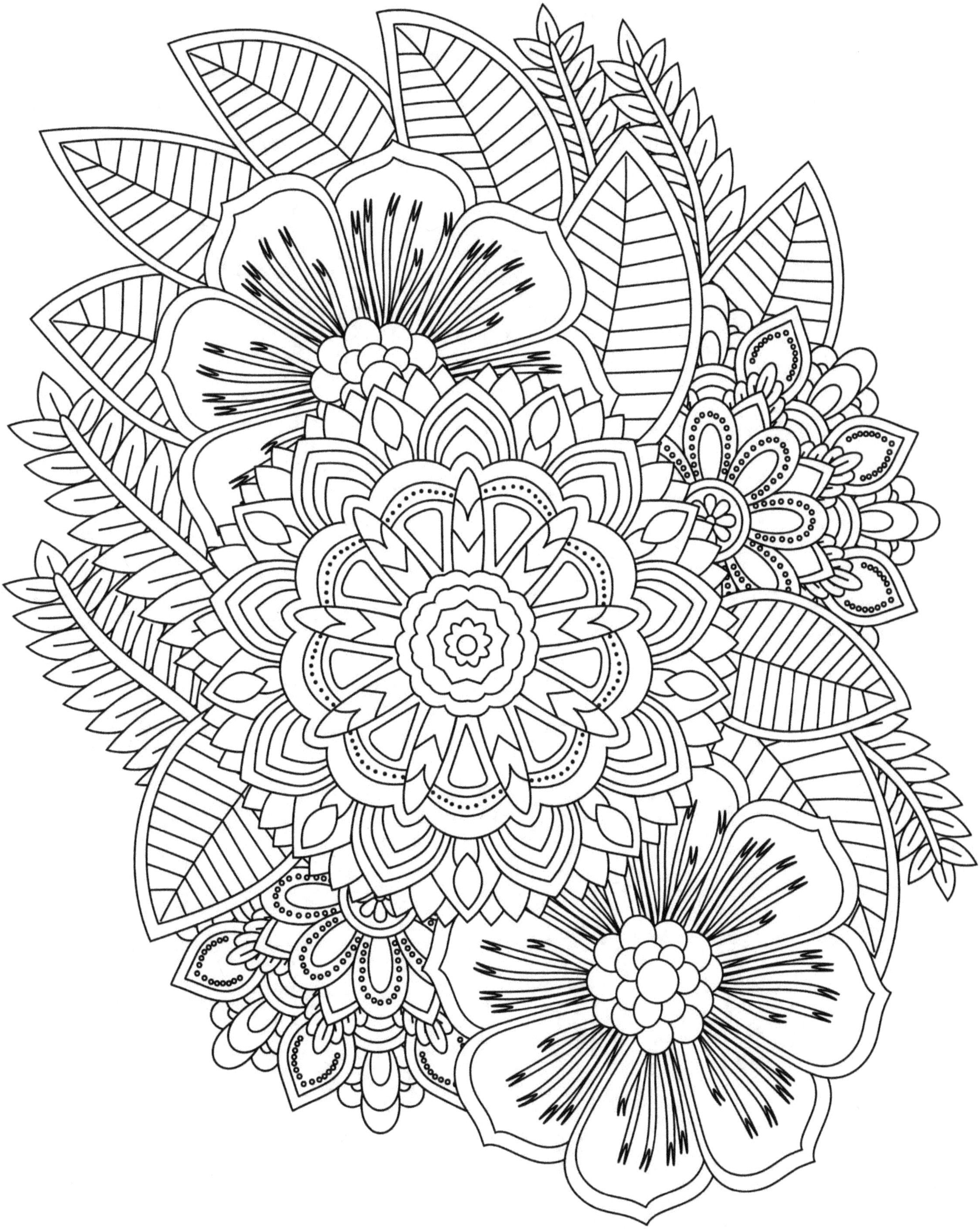

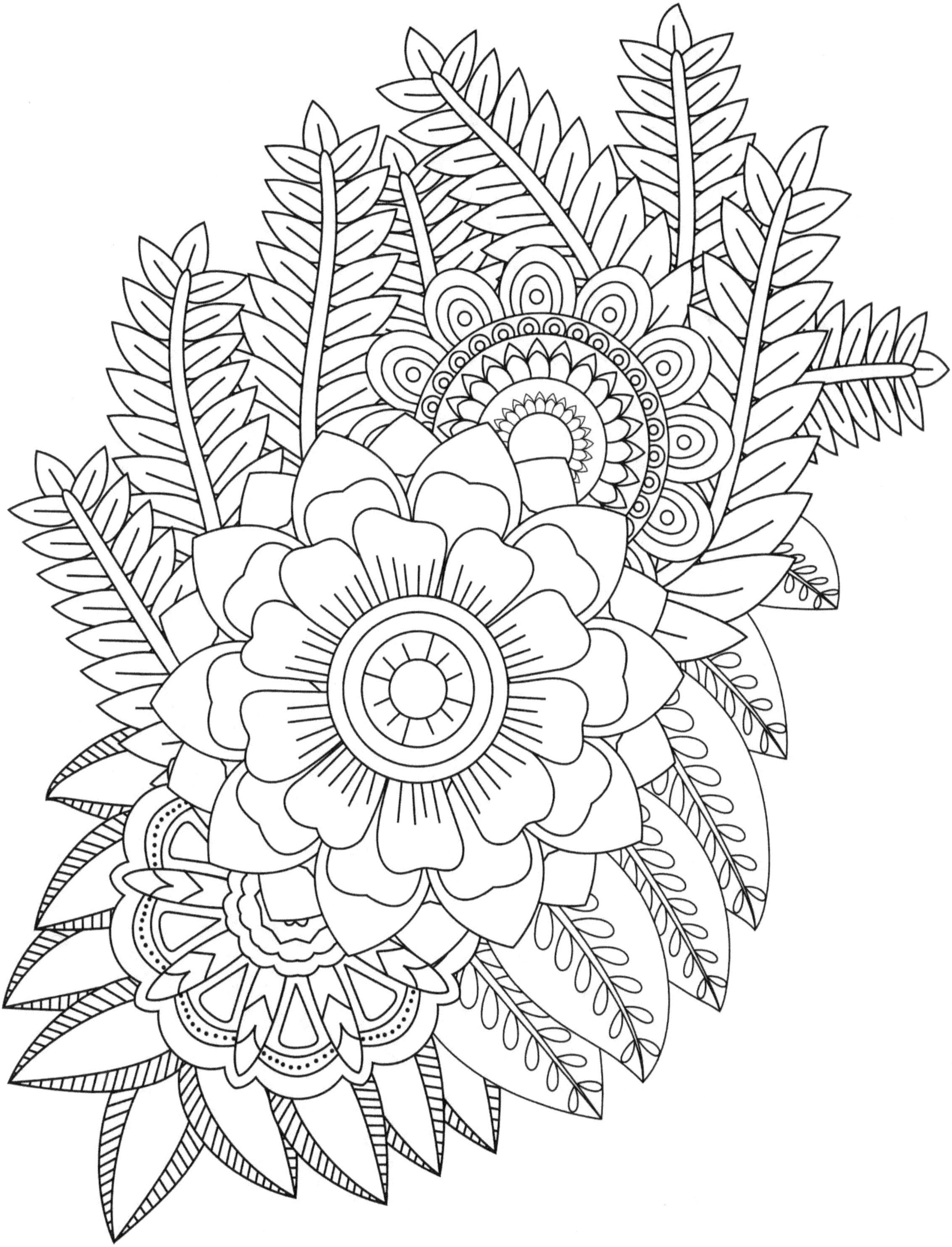

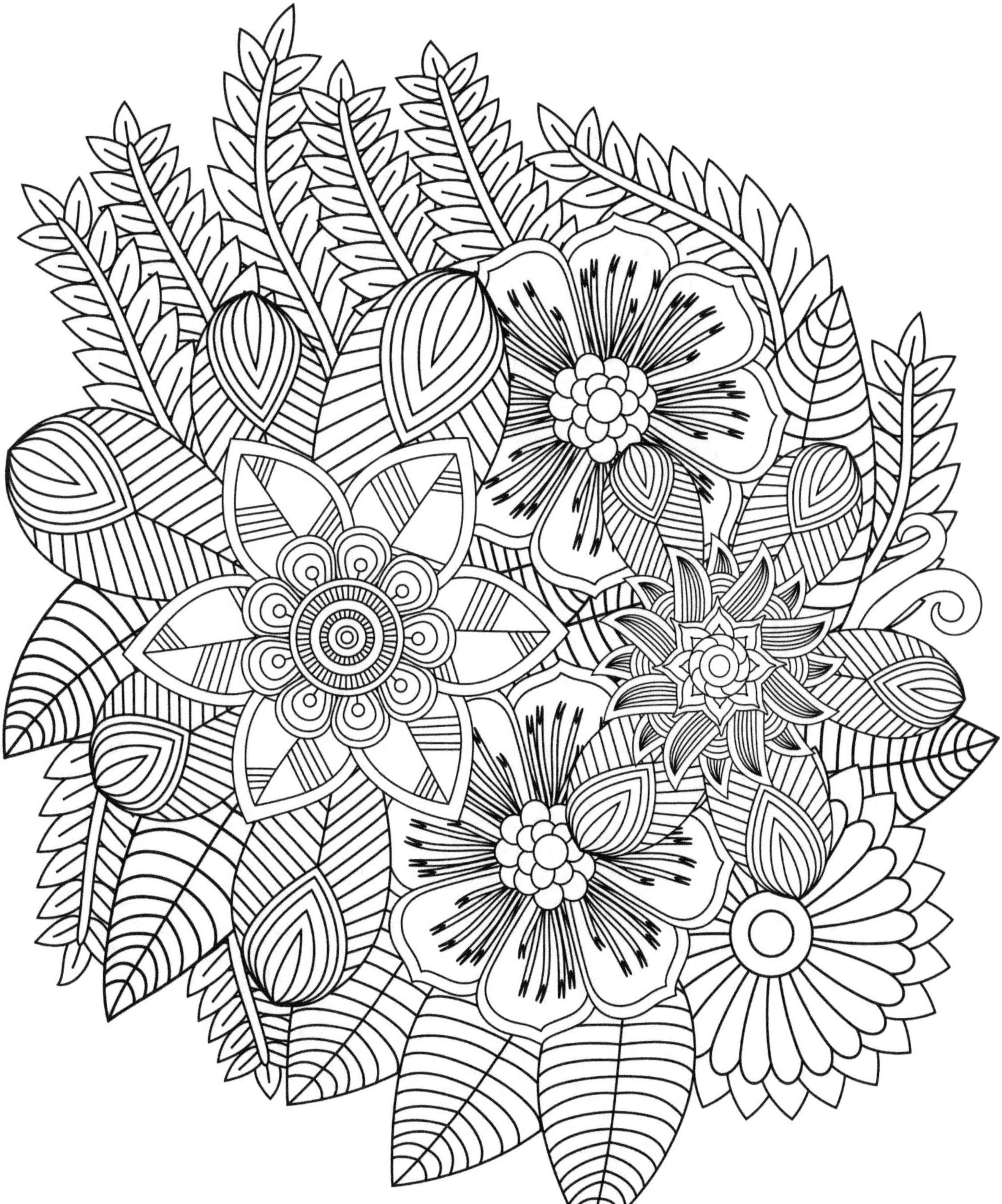

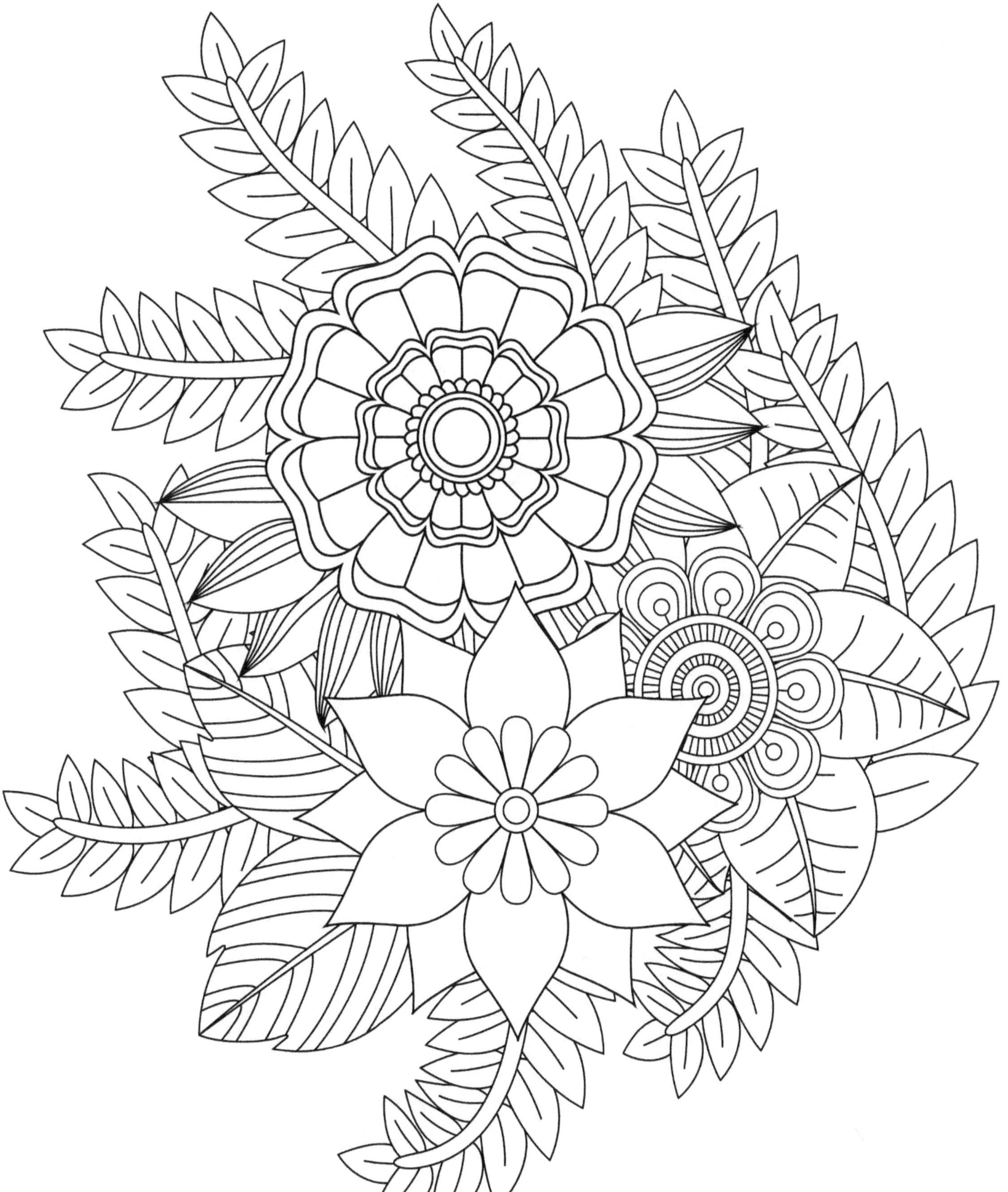

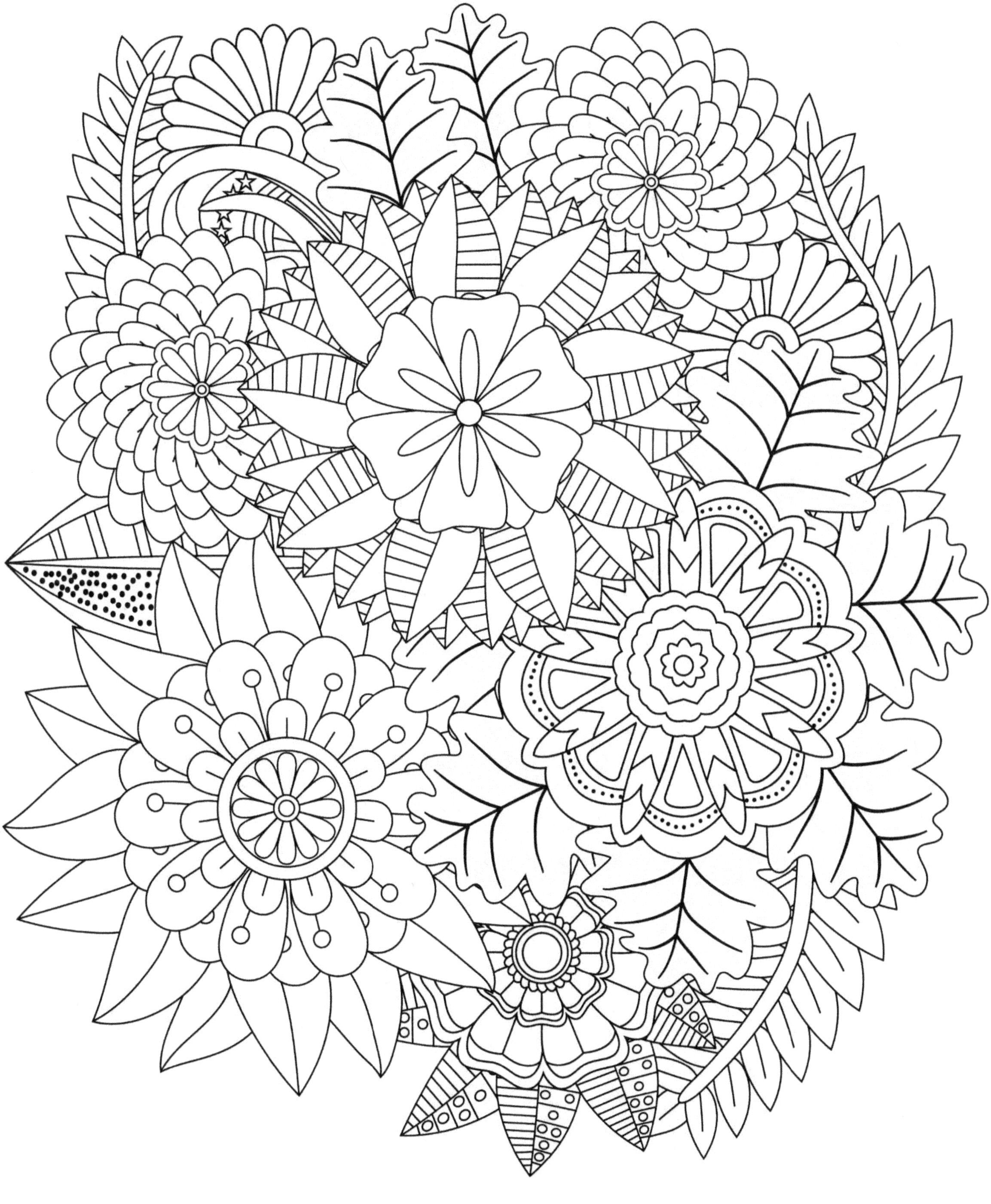

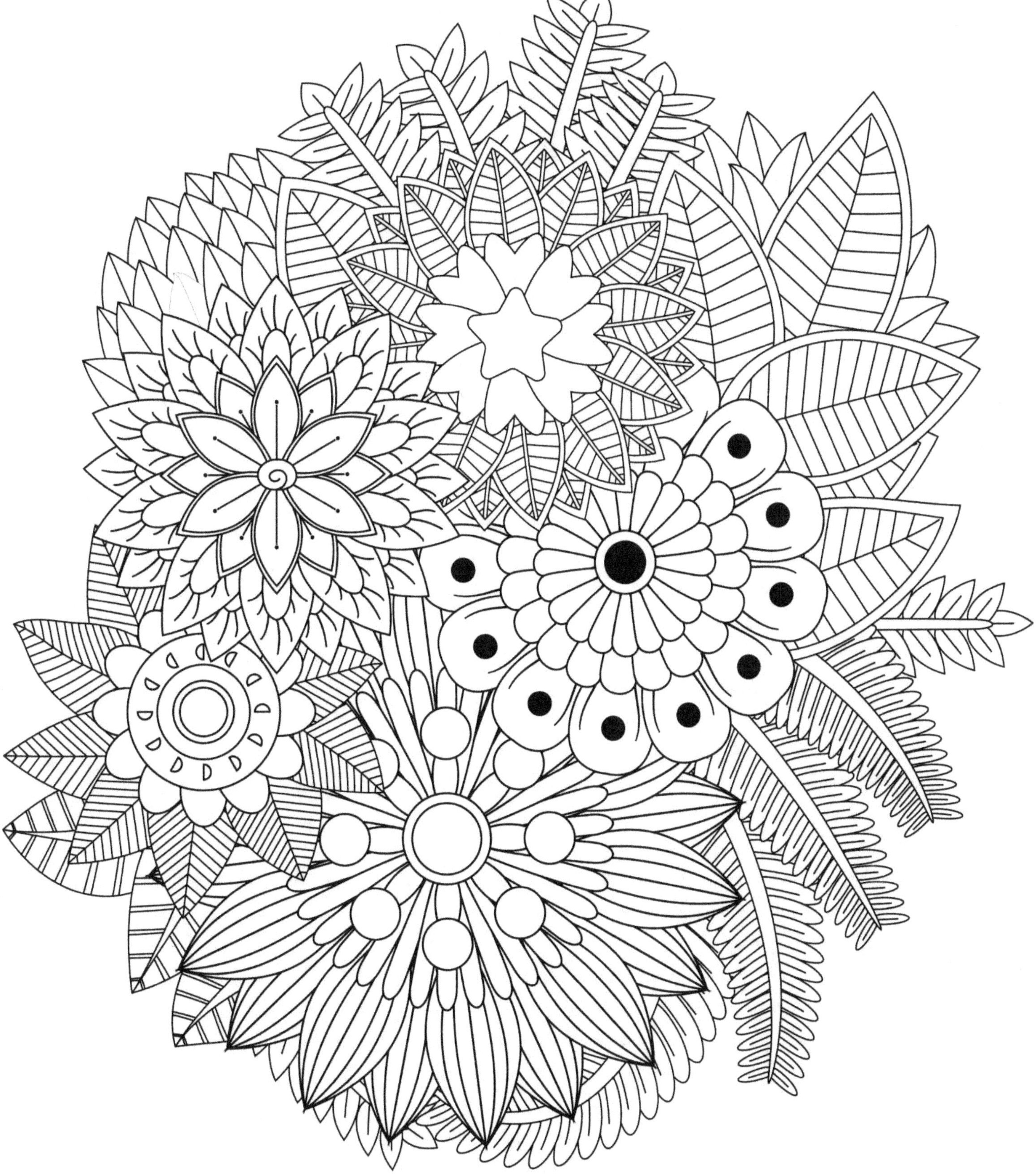

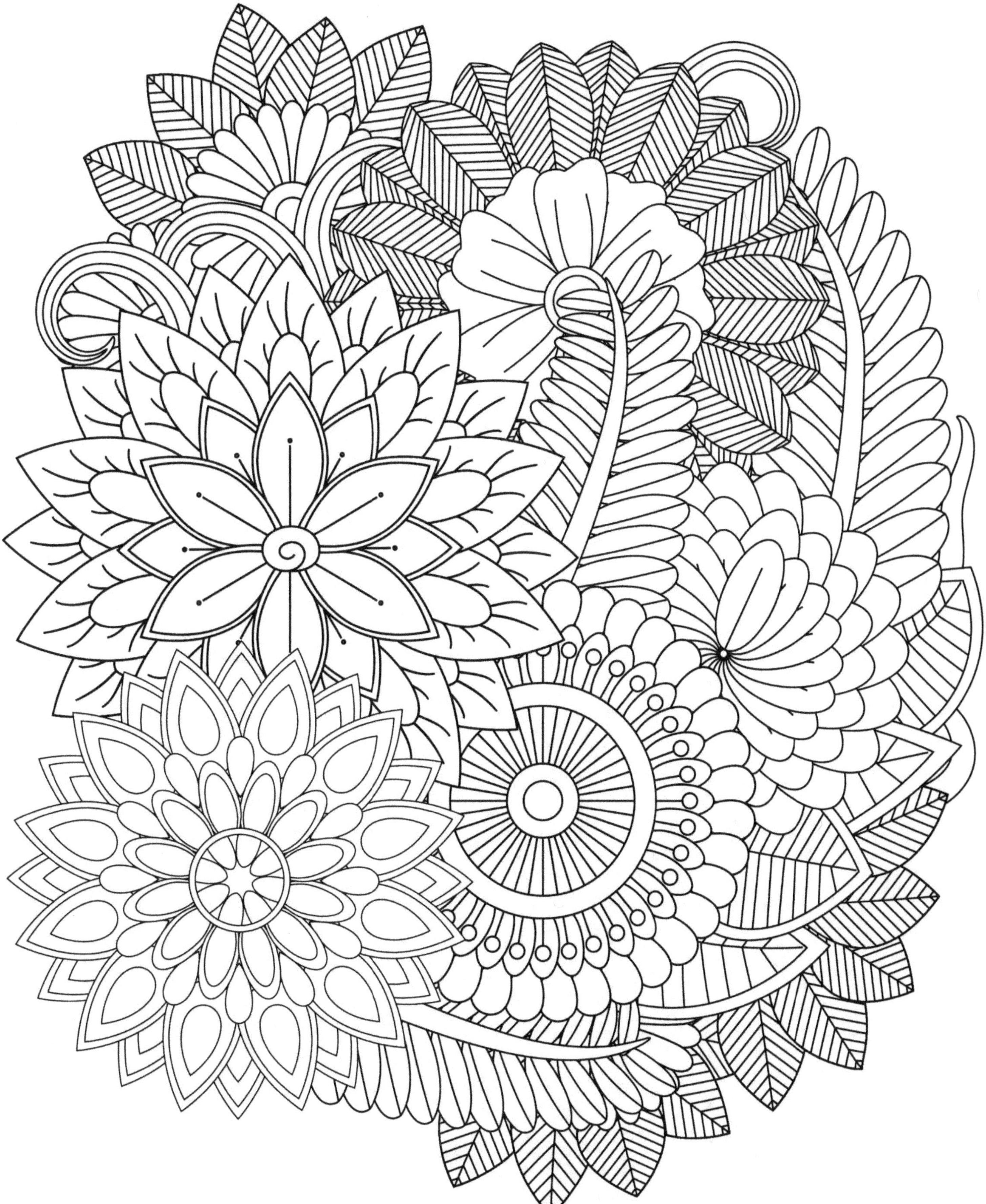

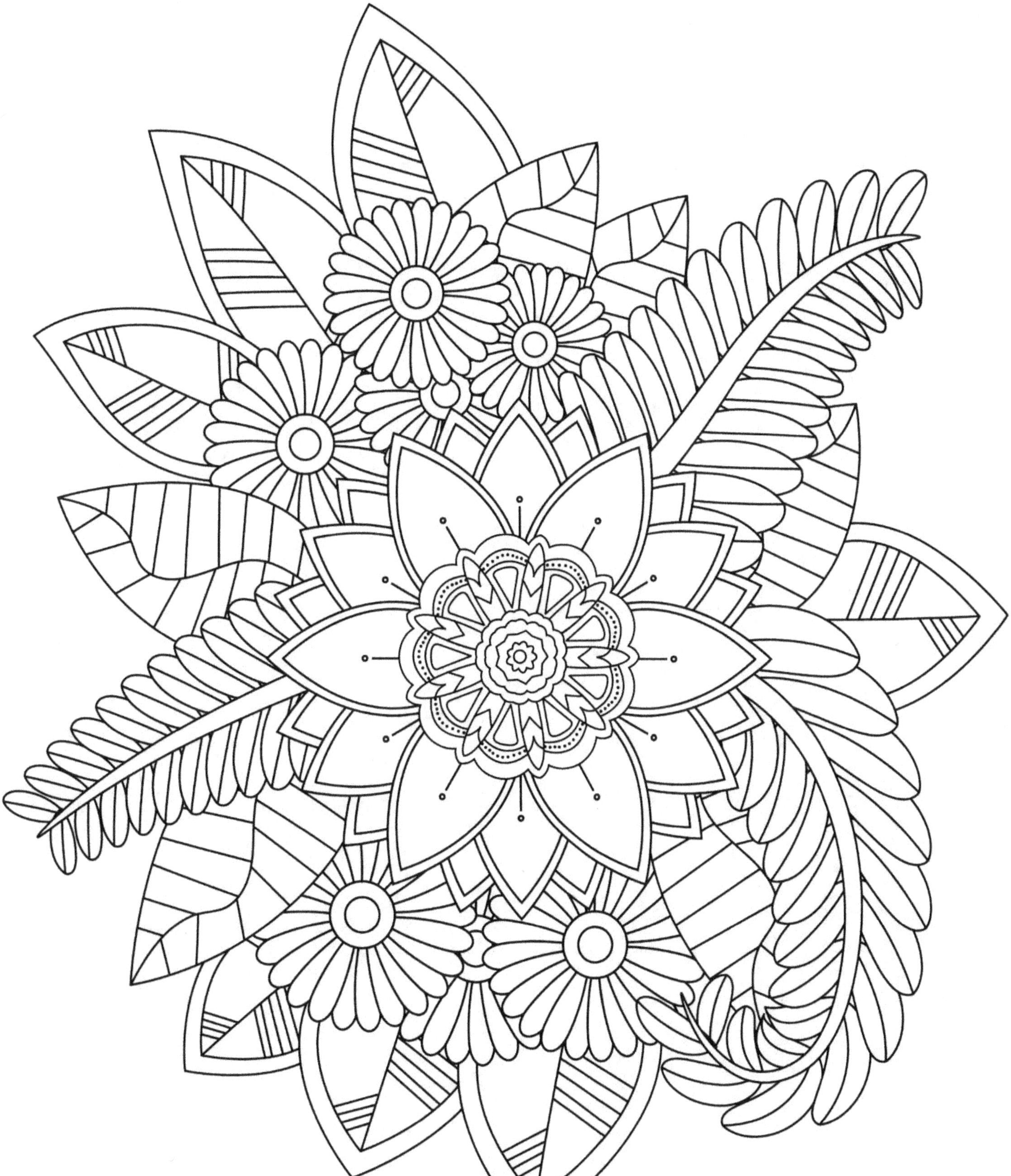

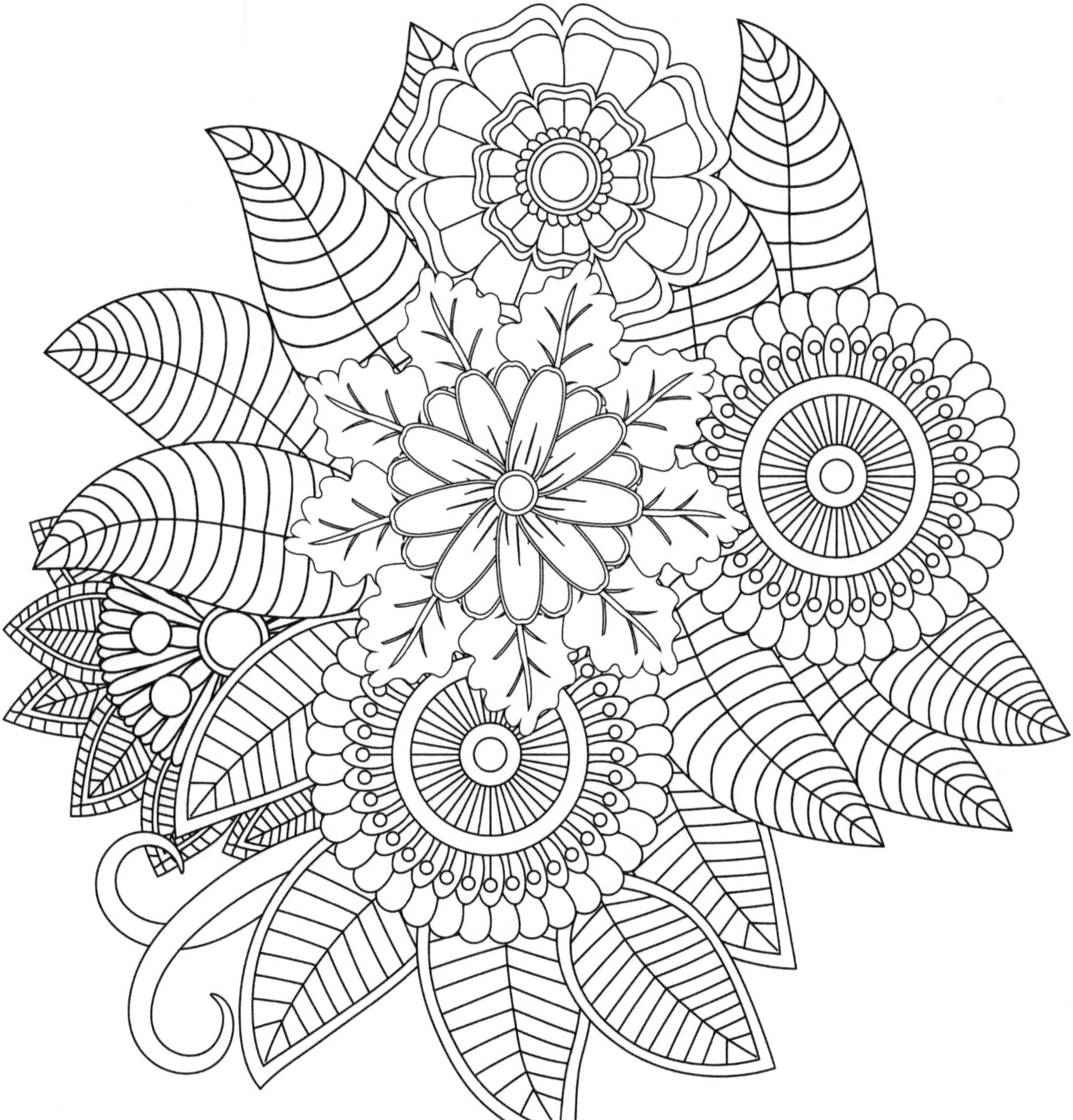

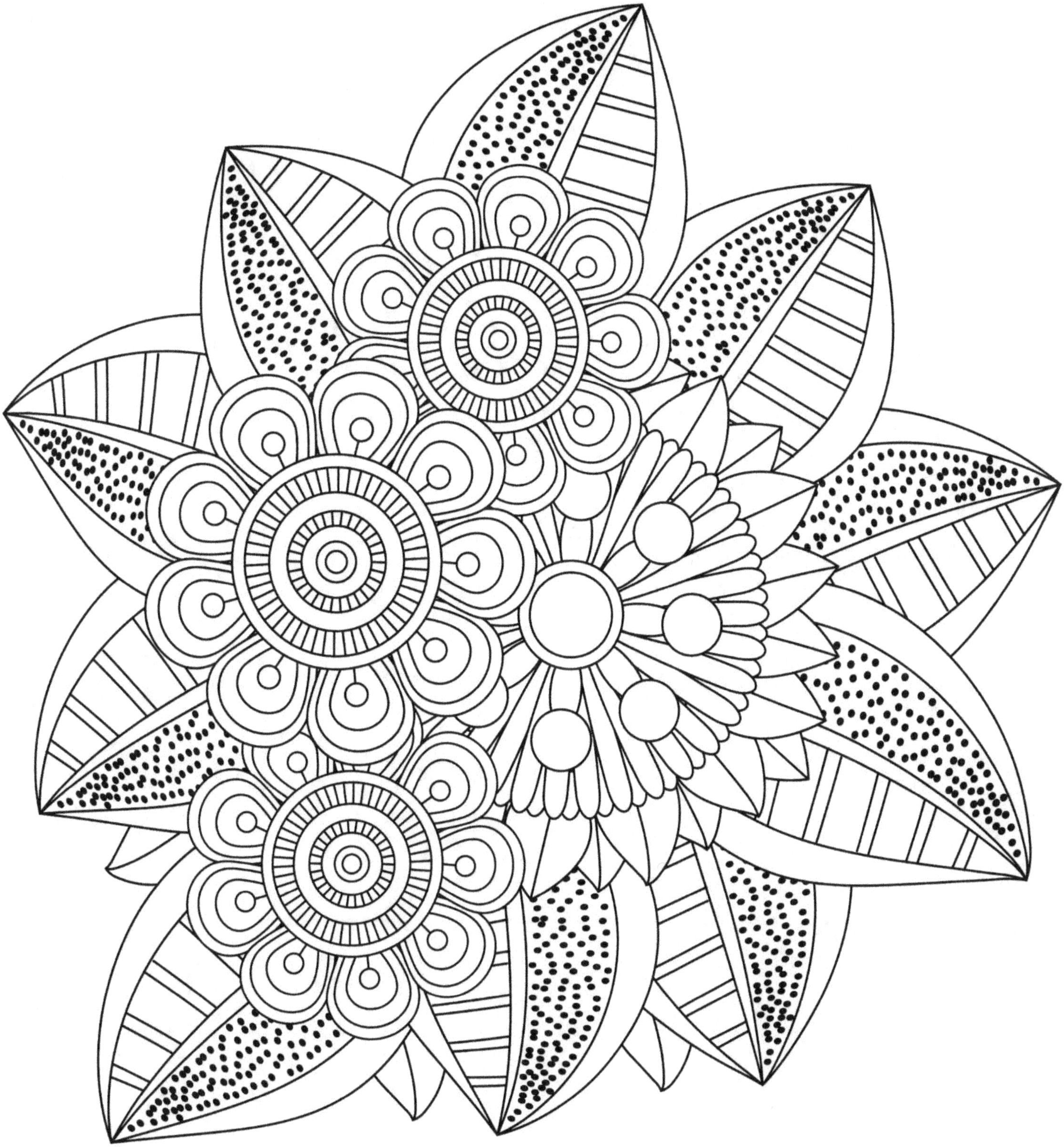

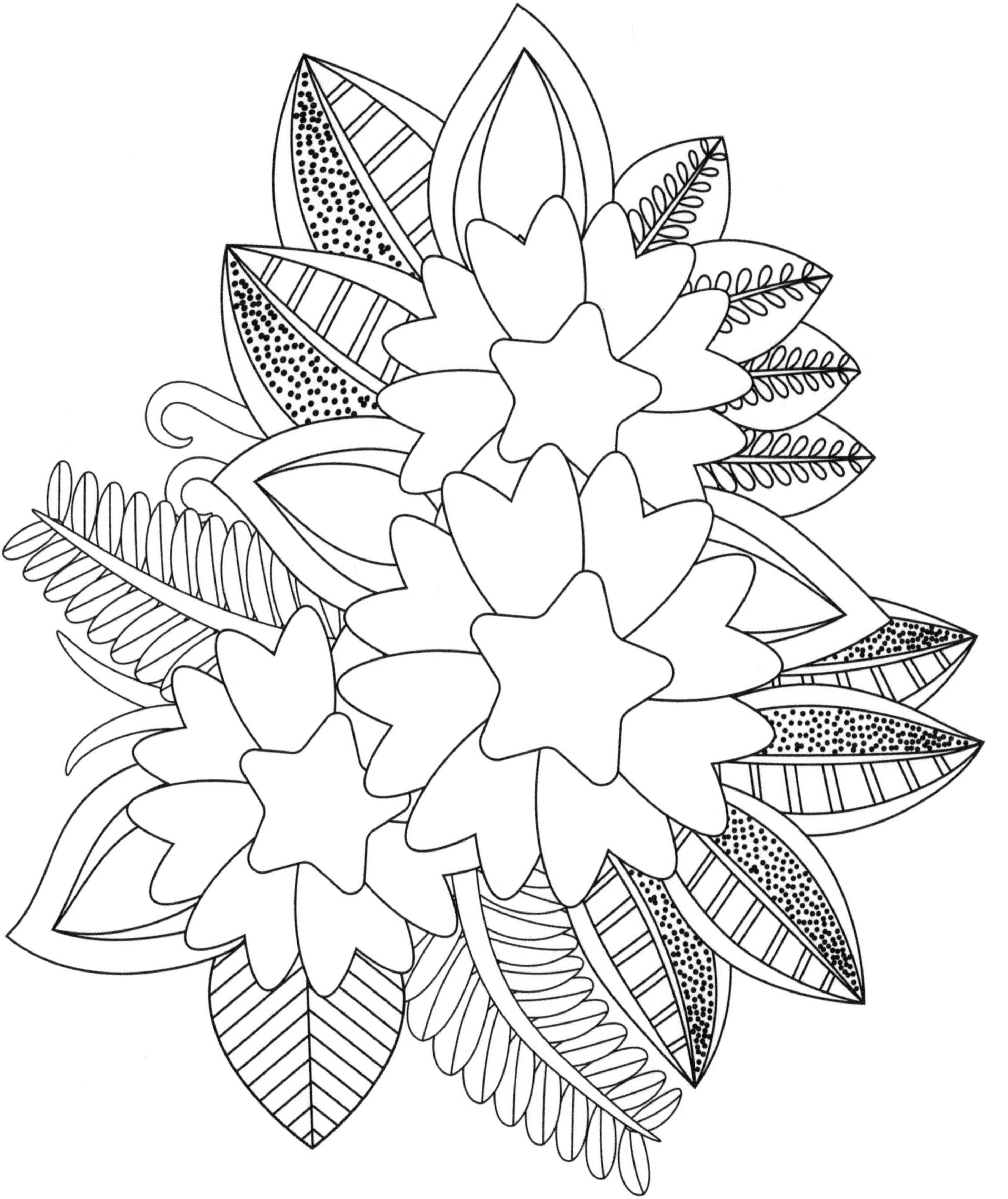

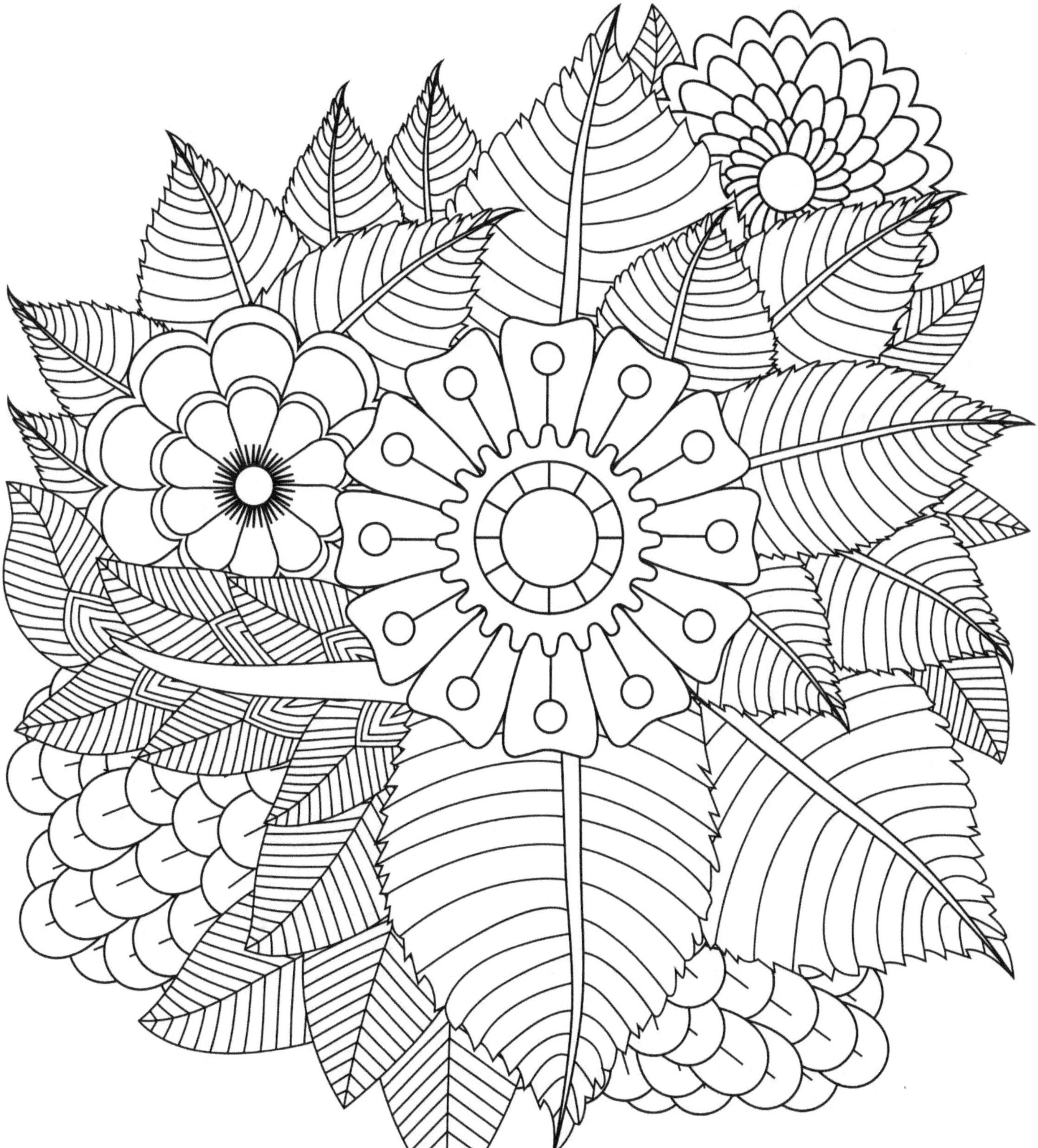

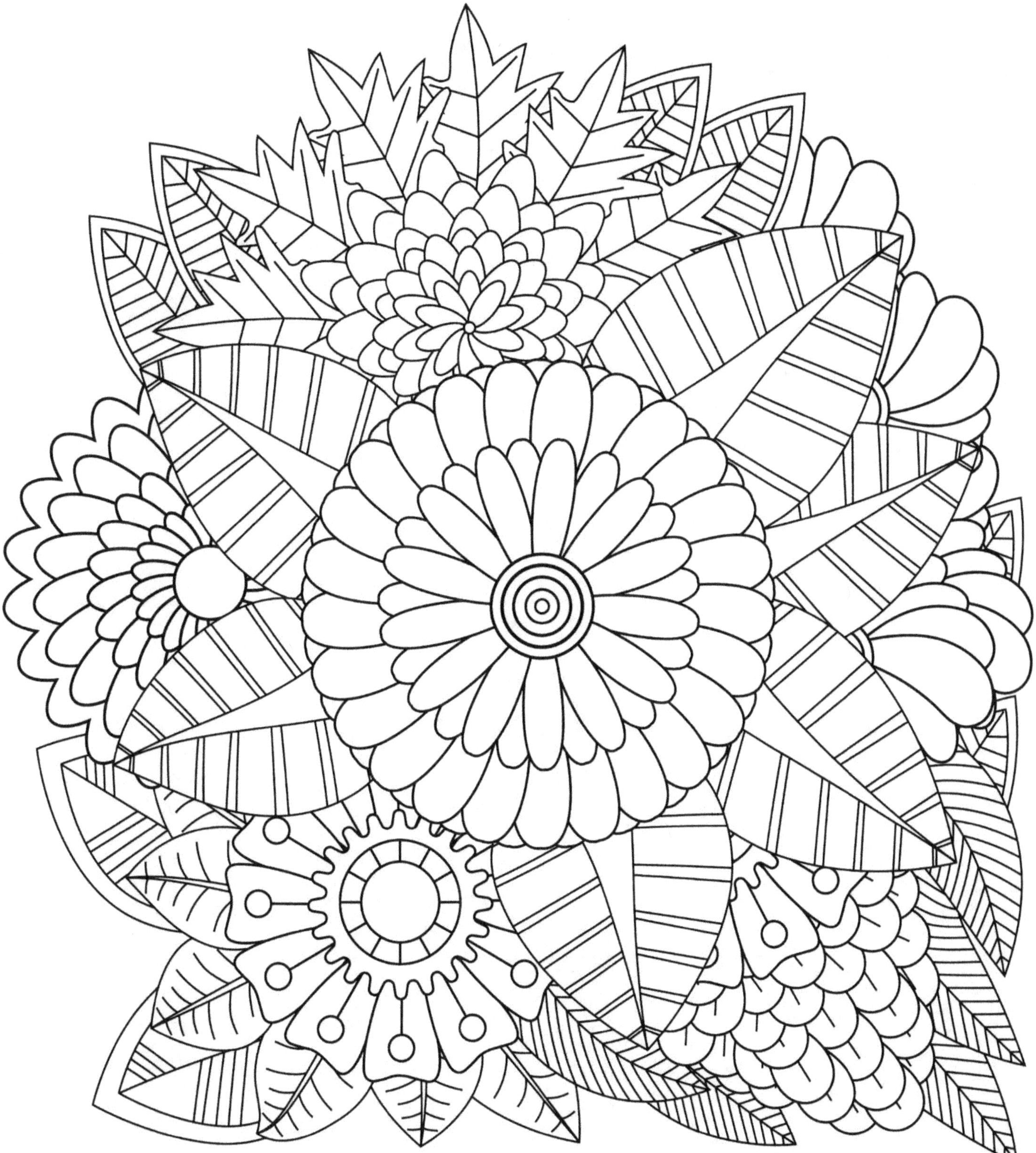

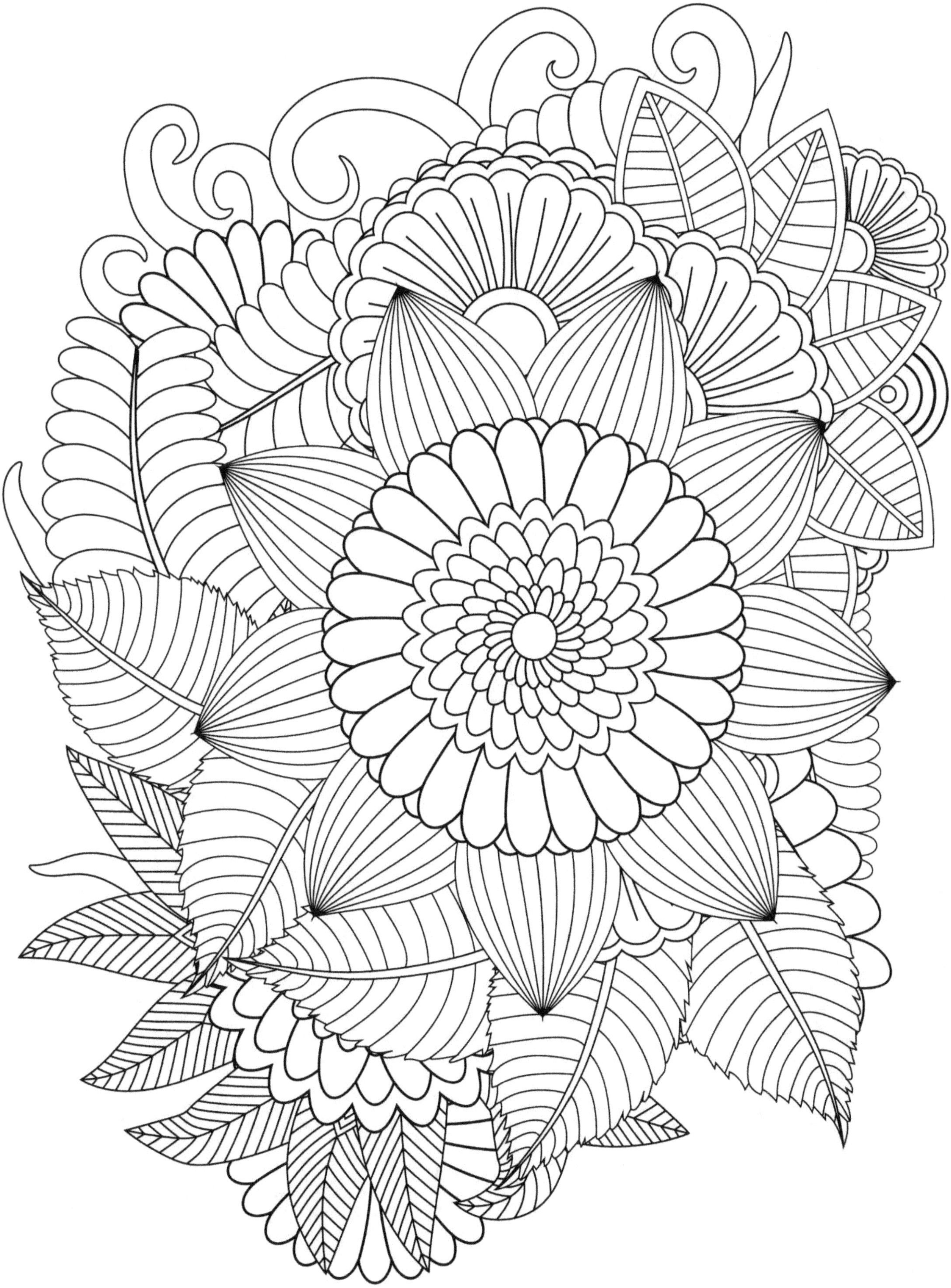

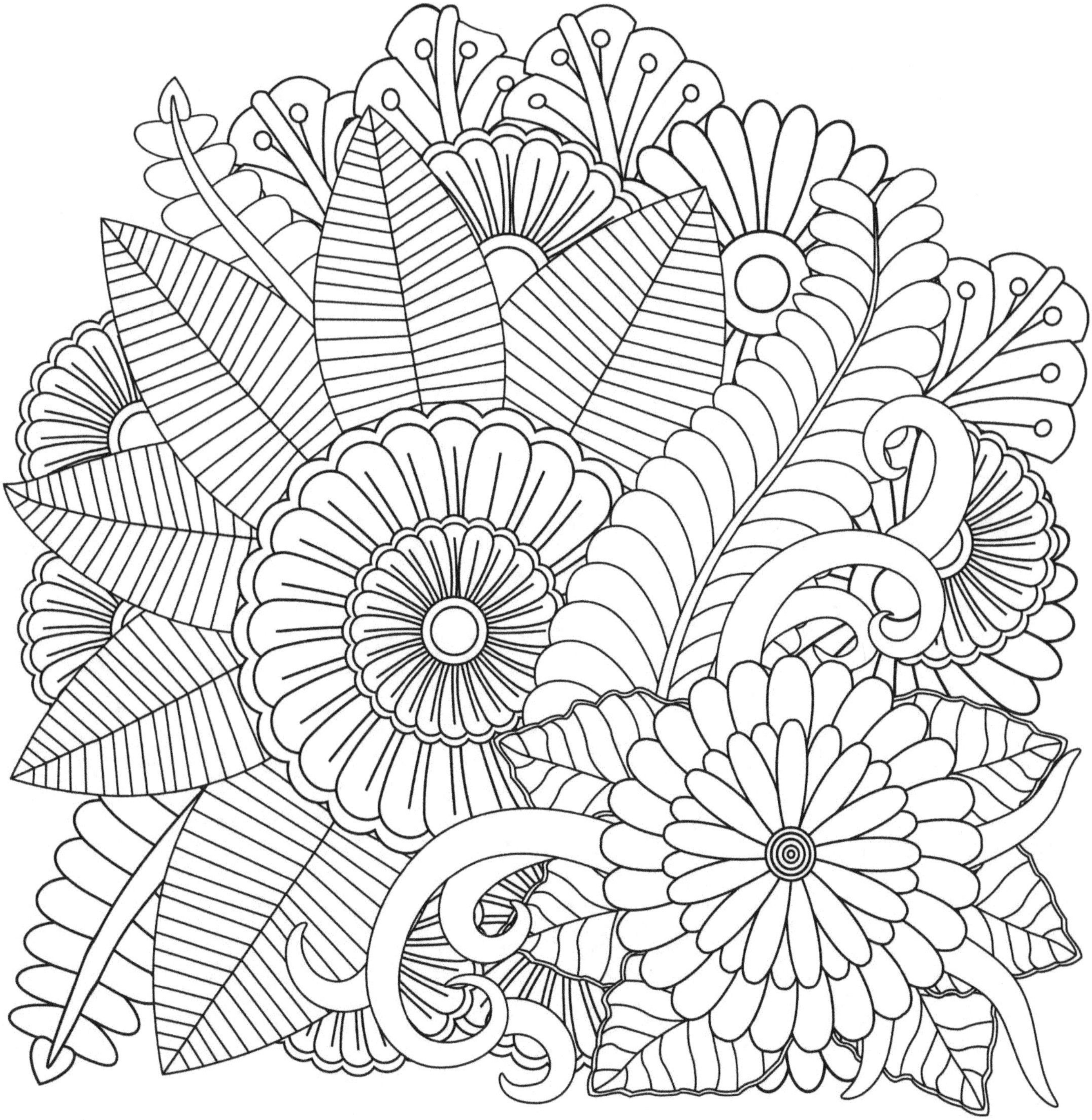

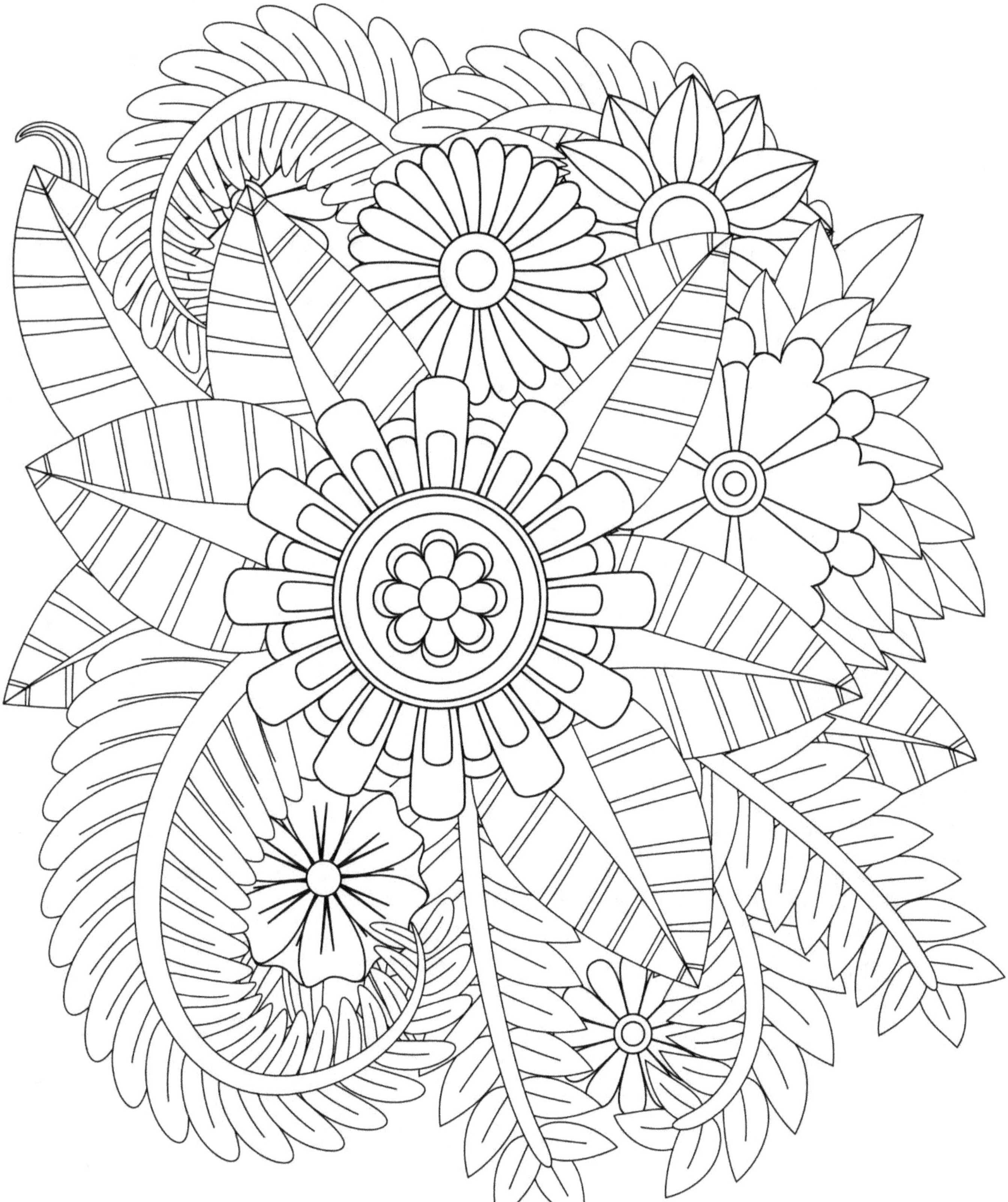

www.ingramcontent.com/pod-product-compliance
Lightning Source LLC
Chambersburg PA
CBHW082113220526
45472CB00009B/2159
* 9 7 9 8 3 2 8 0 1 7 4 1 1 *